RAILWAYS ROUND
DARTMOOR

Bernard Mills

Published in Association with the Dartmoor Trust Archive

First published in Great Britain in 2019
in association with the Dartmoor Trust.
Text and images © Bernard Mills 2019
Historic photos © The Dartmoor Trust Archive unless otherwise stated.

British Library Cataloguing-in-Publication Data.
A CIP record for this title is available from the British Library.

ISBN 978 0 85710 125 9

PiXZ Books
Halsgrove House, Ryelands Business Park, Bagley Road, Wellington,
Somerset TA21 9PZ Tel: 01823 653777
Fax: 01823 216796
email: sales@halsgrove.com

An imprint of Halstar Ltd, part of the Halsgrove group of companies.
Information on all Halsgrove titles is available at: www.halsgrove.com

Printed and bound in India by Parksons Graphics Pvt Ltd

Title page: The view from Lydford looking towards Plymouth in the last weeks of operation. By this time the GWR Launceston Branch together with the wartime connection between the two systems had been lifted. Gibbet Hill the highest point of Blackdown is to the left, in the distance Brentor. 24 April 1968. Above: Crowds celebrate the opening of the South Devon Railway Company's line to Millbay, Plymouth, 1849.

Foreword

This is the second book* in a planned series to promote the Dartmoor Trust Archive by taking particular themes in which to showcase just some of the 25 000 photographs now held in the Archive and which are available to the public through its website at www.dartmoorarchive.org.

Along with the work of the National Park Authority there are many smaller organisations and groups that dedicate their time to ensuring that Dartmoor remains a place in which the natural landscape, the lives of those who live here and those who visit, achieve a harmony in which the essential nature of the environment is conserved. The Dartmoor Trust is one such body, a charity that provides support for local projects and whose members and Trustees appreciate and care about Dartmoor. But in order to best care for the future we must also look to the past, and the Dartmoor Trust Archive, from which many of the photographs in this book are drawn, provides this vital link to our history.

While the earliest photographs held in the Archive date from the dawn of photography, this book in particular gives evidence that photographs need not be very old in order to be important. While the coming of the railways which once encircled the moor was vital in opening up communities and industries to the wider world, their time was comparatively short-lived and much of what existed has now disappeared, their remains barely visible. It is only through photographs such as those taken by the author in the mid twentieth century, just as many of the lines were being dismantled, that we get a picture of the enormous impact the railways once had on the moorland landscape and the legacy that remains. The author's 'before and after photographs' included here just are as important as the rarest and earliest photographs the Archive contains.

The Dartmoor Trust Archive is open to all. I encourage you to explore the Archive online, to add further information to existing images, or to provide photographs of your own. Should you wish to be involved I invite you to contact us – Dartmoor's future is in our hands.

Lt Col. (Retired) Tony Clark OBE
Chairman. The Dartmoor Trust & Archive

*See also *Legendary Dartmoor Pubs and Inns* in this series.

Main line in the National Park: The Northern Moor. 31840 crosses Meldon Viaduct high above the West Okement River with the 1400 Bude–Okehampton. Passengers travelling from the Atlantic Coast once enjoyed a brief view of Dartmoor and the viaduct still stands but sadly only walkers and cyclists cross it today. 29 August 1964.

Main line in the National Park: the Southern Moor. Ex LMS 6233 Duchess of Sutherland heading past Cheston near Wrangaton with 1Z20 0805 London Paddington-Plymouth Great Britain XII. Brent Hill makes a fine backdrop. 27 April 2019.

Contents

Foreword • 3

The Dartmoor Trust Archive • 6

Introduction • 9

The South Devon main line Exeter–Plymouth • 11

The Redlake Tramway • 14

The Zeal Tor Tramway • 20

The Kingsbridge Branch • 22

The Ashburton Branch • 29

The Moretonhampstead Branch • 40

The Haytor Granite Tramway • 49

The Southern Railway main line Exeter–Plymouth • 63

The Fatherford Tramway • 71

Okehampton Military Railways: The Okehampton Target
    Railway East Mill Tor to Skit Bottom • 75

Okehampton Military Railways: Rowtor • 77

The Rattlebrook Peat Railway • 88

The Branch: Plymouth–Tavistock South–Launceston • 105

The Plymouth & Dartmoor Railway • 113

The Princetown Branch • 113

The Lee Moor Tramway • 133

*A Moorland terminus. Ashburton. The Devon Belle Observation Car
number 13 at the rear of the 0945 from Totnes. 2 October 1971.*

The Dartmoor Trust Archive

The Dartmoor Trust itself came about through the foresight of the Dartmoor National Park Authority which, in 1996, saw the advantages of an independent charitable body that, whilst championing the overall aims of the Authority, could undertake projects that were outside the statutory body's remit. In those two decades the Dartmoor Trust, under the guidance of its Trustees, has provided financial support to a wide range of organisations and individuals, from the restoration ancient artefacts to major educational exhibitions. From the outset the Trustees determined to look for a keystone project that would underpin the overall objectives of the Trust, establishing a permanent profile alongside its continuing support for local initiatives. And so the Dartmoor Trust Archive came about – today a sophisticated data platform providing easy public access to over 30 000 images.

Such successes are not achieved without dedication and effort behind the scenes, and alongside their work on other projects the Trustees found themselves engaged in promoting the archive to encourage wider public interest. To this end, in 2000, a book *Dartmoor Century I* was published based on the late Victorian photographs of Robert Burnard. The book was launched accompanied by a major exhibition of photographs, and a year later *Dartmoor Century II* was published to celebrate the addition to the archive of 2300 photographs from the Sydney Taylor Collection. This was followed by the digitisation of the Chapman Collection of 4000 photographs, dating from the Victorian period to the 1960s and, more recently, over 6000 photographs from the Worth Collection held in the Torquay Natural History Museum. The fact that the majority of these thousands of images previously existed in negative form only, many as fragile glass plates, made it almost impossible for the public to have access to them. At last, through carefully

digitising each photograph, it was possible to reveal – often for the first time for many years – thousands of unique images of Dartmoor.

Such work is not without cost, and while the Trust has been assiduous in working within constrained budgets, it has been fortunate in seeking and receiving various generous grants and donations in order to maintain and develop the archive, constantly adding new photographs and upgrading the site and data storage, as the technology develops. In common with most charitable bodies, this era of austerity places severe constraints on finances, with the consequent need to seek further funding in order to continue the Trust's work. Among several new initiatives, the Trustees are publishing a series of books, of which this is the second, each covering a particular theme or aspect of Dartmoor based on images selected from the archive.

Three of the many railway photographs from the Taylor Collection now in The Dartmoor Trust Archive. Left: The Flying Scotsman passing over the summit at Hemerdon returning from service on the Kingswear line on its way to turning on the Laira triangle, 21 September 1973. Above: Brent station in the 1930s. Right: Yelverton station porter, Jim Thomas in the 1940s.

Railways Round Dartmoor

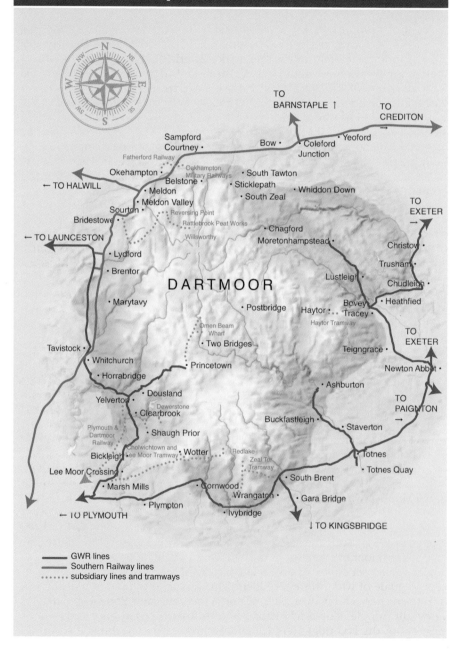

TO
BARNSTAPLE ↑

TO
CREDITON
→

Sampford
Courtney ·
Fatherford Railway

Bow · · Coleford · Yeoford
Junction

Okehampton ·
Oakhampton
Military Railways
Belstone ·
· Meldon
· Meldon Valley
Sourton ·
Reversing Point
Rattlebrook Peat Works
Willsworthy

· South Tawton
· Sticklepath
· South Zeal · Whiddon Down

← TO HALWILL

Bridestowe ·

← TO LAUNCESTON

· Lydford

· Brentor

· Marytavy

Tavistock ·

· Whitchurch

· Horrabridge

Yelverton ·

· Dousland
Dewerstone
· Clearbrook

Plymouth &
Dartmoor
Railway

Bickleigh ·

Lee Moor Crossing ·

· Marsh Mills

Cholwichtown and
Lee Moor Tramway · Wotter ·

· Shaugh Prior

· Plympton

← TO PLYMOUTH

· Chagford
Moretonhampstead ·

Christov ·

Trusham ·

Lustleigh ·

Chudleigh ·

· Heathfied

TO
EXETER
→

DARTMOOR

· Postbridge

Omen Beam
Wharf
· Two Bridges

· Princetown

Haytor · · · Tracey ·
Haytor Tramway

Teigngrace ·

Bovey

TO
EXETER
→

Newton Abbot ·

· Ashburton

Buckfastleigh ·

Redlake
Zeal Tor
Tramway

· Cornwood

Wrangaton ·

· Ivybridge

· Staverton

· Totnes

· Totnes Quay

· South Brent

· Gara Bridge

TO
PAIGNTON
→

↓ TO KINGSBRIDGE

——— GWR lines
——— Southern Railway lines
······· subsidiary lines and tramways

8

Introduction

Dartmoor National Park, created in 1951, is an area of moorland, granite, bogs and craggy tors covering 368 square miles in the county of Devon. When the expanding Victorian railway network arrived in this part of the world, the main line railways chose not to go over the moor but around it, the South Devon Railway (later GWR) taking a southerly course; the London & South Western electing to circumnavigate the northern moor before following the moorland's western flank on its way to the Tavy and Tamar valleys. Both routes made incursions on to the moor but did not stray far inside what today comprises the National Park boundary. It was only from the SDR route that branch lines were built heading in to the moor and only one of these ran on to the High Moor, the much lamented Princetown Branch taking God's Wonderful Railway to its highest point and thus the closest to its creator.

A number of mineral lines some of which predate the main railway era pierced the High Moor. The Haytor tramway, with granite rails carrying that same stone from the quarries, and the Plymouth & Dartmoor both came into being a quarter of a century before the Moor saw its first main line, which the short-lived Zeal Tor Tramway predated by a year. Two further narrow gauge lines penetrated high into the Moor. The 1872 Rattlebrook Peat Railway sought to bring fuel from the northern moor, while the Redlake Tramway of 1911 carried china clay from the south. The military built four small railways above Okehampton and five more on Blackdown, otherwise, with the exception of some minor tramways, it was a region where the railway was otherwise kept at bay.

Today the GWR main line makes a brief passage through the southern Moor on its way from Paddington to the West; while a stub of the former LSWR route at Meldon, on what is now the Dartmoor Railway, crosses the northern boundary. Most of the Ashburton Branch survives as the highly successful South Devon Railway, taking passengers to Buckfastleigh within yards of the National Park. Moretonhampstead has long forgotten its railway, of which only the first third survives as far as Heathfield, its future uncertain at the time of writing.

The Granite Way and Drake's Trail now provide access to the edge of the moor utilising former track beds, The most spectacular cycling and walking route on any former railway must be that from Burrator to Princetown. Perhaps we should be thankful that the industries served by the mineral lines that once scarred the moorland landscape are also now but a memory.

I have in general in kept to the boundary of the Dartmoor National Park created in 1951; taking the reader on an imaginary circular anti-clockwise journey around Dartmoor by train, starting and finishing at Stowford near Ivybridge. This book does not set out to be a complete history of the Dartmoor railways but is a general guide of what was once where. The illustrations are in the main of my own taking or from my own extensive photographic collection where I hold the copyright, supplemented by historic photos from the Dartmoor Trust Archive and that of the Ivybridge Heritage and Archives Group. Pictures from outside sources are credited to the photographer in the caption details.

My thanks are due to many people who have assisted in the preparation of this volume: to Roger Geach for help with pictures and scanning, Barry Jones for help with picture restoration, Stewart Hammond for help with pictures and taking me in search of locations I could not easily find on my own and Jeremy Clark for historical information and help with visits to some remote locations and proof reading. Thanks also to Paul Burkhalter, Ian H. Lane, Brian Mosely and Amayas Crump for additional information, to John Brodribb for information on the Ashburton Branch, my brother-in law-Victor Freeman for advice on matters military, Alan Taylor for providing information on the present-day South Devon Railway and Bovey Tracey station. I also wish to thank Lesley Thatcher of the Ivybridge Heritage and Archives Group, Tom Greeves (Chairman of the Dartmoor Society) who has put me on the trail for further research, and to Simon Butler and his team for their excellent work in producing this volume. A special thank you to my good friend Tony Kingdom who has produced superb books on all the GWR Branches that lead into the Moor and who gave permission to use and quote from his extensive research. So many others have contributed to make this book possible and if I have overlooked anyone please accept my apologies.

Abbreviations used in this book:
BR: British Railways/British Rail
DMU: Diesel Multiple Unit
DVR: Dart Valley Railway
EWS: English Welsh and Scottish Railway,
  later DB Schenker and now DB Cargo UK
GWR: Great Western Railway
GWS: Great Western Society
HST: High Speed train
LMS: London Midland & Scottish Railway
LMT: Lee Moor Tramway
LRO: Light Railway Order

LSWR: London & South Western Railway
OS Ordnance Survey (Maps)
P&D: Plymouth & Dartmoor Railway
PDSWJR: Plymouth Devonport & South
  Western Junction Railway
PRC: Plymouth Railway Circle
PVR: Plym Valley Railway
SR: Southern Railway/British Railways
  Southern Region
SDR: South Devon Railway
SDRT: South Devon Railway Trust
WR: British Railways Western Region

Our anti-clockwise journey around Dartmoor by rail commences at Stowford Bridge just to the east of Ivybridge where the line side fence of the main line forms the southern boundary of Dartmoor. About a mile east from here the line enters the National Park, the A38 Devon Expressway then forming the boundary to a point midway between Bickington and Heathfield. 26 July 2014.

The view from Stowford Bridge as 66 122+70000 Britannia make their way east with 1Z86 1006 Penzance-Bristol Temple Meads Great Britain Rail tour. The train has just crossed Ivybridge Viaduct, the left hand tree growth blocking the view of the structure. The yellow marker to the right of the diesel is the 234¾ mile post, the distance from London Paddington via Bristol and the Weston Super Mare Avoiding Line. The train here is between the original Ivybridge station closed in March 1959 and the new one opened 15 July 1994. 29 April 2015.

The South Devon main line Exeter–Plymouth

History: The main line between Exeter and Plymouth built to Brunel's Broad Gauge of 7feet ¼ inches was opened in stages reaching Totnes on 20 July 1847. Opened 5 May 1848 from Totnes to a temporary station at Laira Green and into Plymouth Millbay 4 April 1849, it is the part of the line between Totnes and Plymouth which is relevant to this volume, in particular travelling from east to west where just before the summit of the climb from Totnes, the railway passes through the 869 yards twin tunnels at Marley. Emerging from the tunnel the line is now within the National Park, and hugs its southern perimeter as it winds its way through Brent, over the summit of the line between Exeter and Plymouth 470 feet above sea level at Wrangaton, thence the gentle descent past Bittaford and Ivybridge leading to the railway exiting the National Park to serve as its southern boundary until near Cornwood.

The Exeter-Plymouth route was planned as a double track main line through-out. However, the SDR became somewhat impoverished and one of the early economies was to construct the route from Rattery to Hemerdon (to the west of Cornwood) as a single line. The South Devon Company was amalgamated with the Great Western Railway as from 1 February 1876. The GWR inherited it must be said a well maintained line but one with capacity issues due to the long single line sections. Over the weekend of 20-23 May 1892, all remaining Broad Gauge lines west of Exeter were converted to the standard gauge of 4 feet 8½ inches in one fell swoop, the GWR then turning its attention to increasing speed and easing the bottlenecks, in chronological order the route was doubled as follows: Rattery-Brent (including a second single bore Marley Tunnel) and Cornwood-Hemerdon 14 May 1893, Ivybridge to Blatchford 11 June 1893, Wrangaton-Ivybridge 13 August 1893, Brent-Wrangaton 8 October 1893 Blachford-Cornwood 19 November 1893. The line passed to British Railways on nationalisation 1 January 1948. The botched railway privatisation of the 1990s brought the route at first under the ownership of Rail Track as from 1 April 1994, for the sorry story that followed (well beyond the terms of reference of this volume) it turned out to be an appropriate date. On the collapse of Rail Track, the Government owned Network Rail assumed ownership of the national system as from 3 October 2002. The line remains open as part of the Paddington-Penzance route, its intermediate stations closing. 2 March 1959.

The second Ivybridge station looking towards Plymouth, built half a mile to the east of the original due to modern day regulations; we will call in there as we complete our circular tour of Dartmoor by train. 43025 front and 43165 rear pass with 1A85 1100 Penzance-London Paddington. Passengers would now be enjoying their journey beneath the high peaks of the southern moor, the 1095 feet of the tor known as Western Beacon, soon followed by its neighbour the 1223 feet Ugborough Beacon, it is to the summit of the former we now proceed. 26 July 2014.

This is the spectacular view from the top of Western Beacon looking south. It is where the southern tors of Dartmoo rise steeply in grand fashion from rural pastures that border the lush countryside of the South Hams. In terms of the GWR main line this is about a mile to the east of the present-day Ivybridge station.

From this prominent spot below the summit of the Beacon we are looking down on the former Redlake Tramway where it once began its seven-mile journey deep into the central moor. The solitary tree (1) to the bottom right of the photograph provides a marker to discern the tramway's course running across the picture from left to right. Observe behind it the remains of a bridge (2) which carried a track from a nearby quarry (supplying ballast to the tramway) over the incline which connected the tramway with the Cantrell clay works and dryers below – the latter marked by its still extant chimney and the former siding where traffic was interchanged with the GWR. Officially known as Redlake Siding, this opened in June 1912 and closed with its signal box on 7 July 1932. Note the GWR main line to the bottom left of the picture (3).

The buildings at the former Cantrell works survive. For many years they were the home of the Western Machinery Company, and remain in use as the Redlake Industrial Estate adjacent to the B3213 road, the former A38. The dual carriageway Ivybridge bypass of the early 1970s is hidden by the trees just beyond. Of the incline itself, the picture does show that other than a few clues at its summit, no trace of it remains and thus in the present day there is no obvious link between the empty track bed high above the now bustling industrial estate. 2 June 2018.

The Redlake Tramway

The History: This 3 foot gauge line had a life of just over 20 years and was constructed by The China Clay Corporation (its offices in Ivybridge) to serve its china clay quarry high on the desolate moor five miles from the nearest road. It opened on 11 September 1911 and closed in 1932 due to the failure of the Company, the track removed in 1934.

Route: The southern terminus was at the top of a 2210 foot cable-operated 1-in-5 incline which rose 300 feet from the GWR main line at the west end of Cantrell Siding. It ran for 7½ miles and ascended from 400 feet above sea level taking a circuitous course to the High Moor to the clay workings at Redlake 1400 feet above sea level. The track bed remains and is popular with walkers and hikers enabling access to a number of the southern tors such as Sharp Tor and Three Barrows. Along the way are many reminders of the industrial past. The most visible railway relic is the stone bridge at Left Lake. At Redlake itself, now difficult to reach due to the final half mile or so of the tramway course being overgrown and very soggy, the china clay pits are now flooded. For the more ambitious walkers, the route forms the southern section of the Two Moors Way, this extending 102 miles from Ivybridge to the north coast at Lynmouth on Exmoor.

Outward to Redlake in the morning the train would convey workmen and trucks of coal for the pumping engine at Redlake, returning in the evening with the workmen and sand. The clay was piped down, and remains of the pipeline can still be discerned. Fare-paying passengers were never officially carried, although it is known the odd hiker cadged a lift!

Motive Power: The line was steam worked; first on the scene was 0-4-2 C A Hanson, named after the owner. It was built by Kerr Stuart as a 3-foot gauge version of their standard Waterloo class, but instead of the wheels being outside the frames they were inserted inside. Next on the scene was Dartmoor, built by Kerr Stuart. Otherwise not much else is known of it. Lastly was Lady-Mallaby Dee-  ley, a peculiar contraption being a 0-4-0 vertical boiler engine built by Atkinson Walkers. None survived beyond the closure of the line.

Other than an empty track bed, physical reminders of the Redlake Tramway are few. Referring to the view from the top of Western Beacon (p.16), the Tramway extended from the summit of the incline about 300 yards to the east above Bittaford, and here two relics of the line can be found. From the farm gate, where the track bed passes into a field, there are the remains of what was the carriage shed and immediately behind this stands the former locomotive shed (above), built of brick on stone foundations with probably a corrugated roof. Despite not serving its original purpose for over 80 years and its exposed position on the eastern flank of Western Beacon, part of it has survived the effects of the Dartmoor climate, its concrete floor intact although the inspection pit filled in. The end walls and the cast-iron window frames are long gone; the ruined structure standing as a shrine to the railway it once served. 2 June 2018.

Through the Ivybridge Heritage and Archives Group comes the photograph (below) of 0-4-2 tank locomotive *C A Hanson* in an obviously posed picture during shunting operations at the head of the incline up from Cantrell. The engines always faced Redlake so we are looking towards Bittaford with the line leading to the carriage and engine sheds behind. Note the third wagon from the engine is standing (at right angles) on the wagon turntable which gave access to the incline, the latter out of camera range to the right. The tramway's freight rolling stock was made up of a dozen unbraked five ton coal trucks and a similar number of five ton sand trucks, painted in a bluish grey livery. All were built to the same design being four plank wagons with, as can clearly be seen in the picture, bottom hung side doors for transferring purposes and they all carried the letter C on their sides. The railway did not convey the mineral it was built to serve, this was piped down from Redlake. The Tramway was in effect the support and lifeline for an industry working quite literally in the middle of nowhere. The building to the left of *C A Hanson* is the incline winding engine house. Undated.

The updated view does indeed show a much changed scene with, other than the track bed, little evidence of this being where the incline once exchanged its traffic with the tramway. Looking to the right, behind the second boulder is the start of the incline. The curve of the wide expanse of what is now a moorland track is an indication there was once a loop here. Behind the bushes to the left is the former site of the incline winding house. 31 August 2014.

The view from Western Beacon looking west, the course of the tramway discernable as it climbs around Leatherdon Hill. The route was superbly engineered by Hansford Worth, winding its way past the Tors following the contours. Although several embankments and cuttings were necessary, there were no major engineering works of note. 2 June 2018.

Just over five miles along the Tramway is Left Lake, the only intermediate point served by the line. A small clay works here was re opened in 1922 and a crossing loop installed. The view is from the spoil tip looking east towards Cantrell with the most notable feature of the tramway to survive, the stone and brick bridge, so well was the line engineered this was the only masonry construction required. 31 May 2018.

Brown Heath is remote, standing about 50 yards or so up from where the course of the Tramway parts Company with the Two Moors Way. I stand in the remains of the Greenhill mica beds and look directly across the open moor to the spoil heap, now reclaimed by nature, at Redlake, the end of the line reached by a semi-circular and now very boggy curve. Within ten minutes of taking this photograph, the Dartmoor mist came down without warning and almost immediately visibility was reduced to a matter of yards. 31 May 2018.

Opposite top: After our excursion to Redlake, we return to the GWR main line about ¼ miles to the east of the former Cantrell Siding. All appears to be quiet on what was then the A38 before the dual carriageway Ivybridge bypass of 1973 took the road on a more southerly course. The B&B sign was in a good position to tempt the weary traveller off the main road. To the right the signpost points to the former Moorhaven Hospital, closed in 1992 since redeveloped as a residential village. Crossing Bittaford Viaduct is the unusual combination of Class 42 Warship D864 *Zambesi* + former GWR Prairie 4555 + two preserved coaches on their way from Buckfastleigh to a BR Open Day at Laira Depot. Just prior to crossing the viaduct, the train would have passed through the former Bittaford Platform opened 18 November 1907 and closed 2 March 1959 of which no trace remains. 25 September 1970.

Opposite lower: A mile and seven chains east of Bittaford Platform lay Wrangaton, the station built in a cutting at the summit of the line between Exeter and Plymouth 442 feet above sea level. It was also built at the junction of the road from Kingsbridge with the Exeter-Plymouth Turnpike, this being at the road bridge we see behind *Castle Class* 5075 *Wellington* passing with a Plymouth-bound train. To the top right is the Kingsbridge Road Hotel, an historic name reflecting the former role of the station originally named Wrangaton, changed after local pressure one year after opening to become Kingsbridge Road. It was a natural point for trains to connect with the stagecoach service to Kingsbridge and was a busy place in its day. On the opening of the Kingsbridge Branch from Brent in 1893, the station reverted to its original name and lost its importance and much of its traffic, thereafter served by local stopping trains until closed 2 March 1959. To the top left on the A38 note the garage and still extant houses which make up most of the hamlet. Sadly the pub, having for a while been named The Wounded Soldier, is now no more, serving as residential accommodation. Just beyond the road bridge, the rear of the train has just made its exit form the short 69-yard Wrangaton Tunnel. 18 May 1959.

On the curve approaching Brent we see 47 237+ former LMS *Black 5* 44932 working 1Z39 1745 Par–Bristol Temple Meads Royal Duchy. This bridge at the western end of the former Brent station is on the road which leads to Shipley Bridge, here one can leave the car in the Avon Dam car park and from there explore the next railway we encounter on our journey east, the Zeal Tor Tramway. 1 September 2013.

The Zeal Tor Tramway

One of the shorter railways of Dartmoor in both lifespan and length is the Zeal Tor Tramway, opened in 1847 from the peat beds at Redlake following a south-easterly course to a naphtha works at Shipley Bridge. The 3½-mile line was worked by horse, wagons pulled along the steeply graded line of wooden rails bolted to granite sleepers. This attempt to bring industry to the wild High Moor was short lived, and as far as I can ascertain, the line had a working life of not more than five years, probably less. Buildings at Shipley Bridge were repaired and re-used by the Brent Moor Clay Company from 1872, this again was short lived allowing peace to return to this part of Dartmoor. I only ever walked the course of most of the Tramway back in April 1968, takingthis picture of the track bed on Bala Brook Heath; one of the few tangible reminders of the line can be spotted to the left, the small granite mound is the ¾ mile post which I told survives to this day and the scene is little changed (inset: enlarged milepost). A challenging walk of about ten miles which can be done in either direction is to walk this line out to Redlake and then back along the Redlake Tramway, or vice versa. Be warned: the course of the Zeal Tor Tramway is not so well defined and is a sterner test for those on foot.

Three miles and twenty three chains east from Wrangaton once lay Brent Station, sited in the village of South Brent; the SDR for some unknown reason ignoring the prefix. The roadside station opened on 15 June 1848 serving the local community. It gained a signal box in 1875 installed here for the crossing loop to give greater flexibility on what was then a single track main line. It became a junction on the opening of the Kingsbridge Branch on 19 December 1893 thus enjoying a much enhanced status, and a new signal box with a 61 lever frame. After the closure of the Kingsbridge Branch on 16 September 1963, it reverted to its role as a wayside station. However, the local patronage was deemed insufficient for its retention and the station closed on 5 October 1964.

This splendid view is by Doug Ellis looking towards Plymouth in the transition period from steam to diesel as 4555 and a brake van pause at the down, i.e. Plymouth-bound platform, with a GWR Toad goods brake van, probably prior to making its way down the branch to collect any freight traffic. In the foreground D6339 is shunting the yard by the cattle pens, probably working the daily Newton Abbot–Ivybridge and return goods. Summer 1962.

The Kingsbridge Branch

This was not really a Dartmoor Railway; it was by an accident of railway geography that the station, where it made its junction with the main line, happened to be situated within the National Park. Once out of the platform and past its main line connection, the branch headed away south in the opposite direction away from the Tors and the wilderness towards the pastoral charm of the Avon Valley, and once over the hill at Sorley down to the heart of the South Hams at Kingsbridge. It was only the first mile of the route that lay in Park, but that is enough to warrant its inclusion when discussing Railways Round Dartmoor.

History: The South Hams felt the need for a railway, but was not that enthusiastic about actually backing it with hard cash, a couple of schemes had been mooted and the second of these actually saw work commence in 1867 only to cease four years later with little action and a lack of finance. A third scheme started in 1885 again suffered the same problems with money until the GWR stepped in and took over with the standard gauge 12 miles and 35 chain route opening on 19 December 1893. It was at times a busy line but very susceptible to road competition; the South Hams looked more towards its road connections to Totnes and Plymouth which by the 1930s were making serious inroads to the railway. The line was very busy with freight and did retain a good volume of local traffic. On summer Saturdays it could carry 1000 passengers in each direction as holidaymakers headed to and from the coast. Indeed through carriages were run to London Paddington a week before the line closed completely on16 September 1963. It was an early candidate for preservation; the late TWE Roche and the Great Western Society recognising the potential. Talks were held soon after the closure between interested parties and sympathetic local BR management. The commercial arm of BR was more interested in lifting the track to realise the income from the scrap rail and anything else that could be sold off. A case of the right hand not knowing what the left hand was doing, people left a meeting with BR in November 1963 only to greet the scrap man on his first day of destroying the line. It all thus came to nothing and attention was turned to support others in their efforts to save the Ashburton Branch and the rest, as they say, is history.

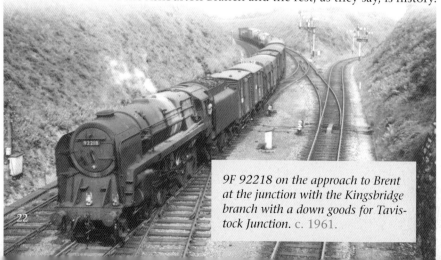

9F 92218 on the approach to Brent at the junction with the Kingsbridge branch with a down goods for Tavistock Junction. c. 1961.

We head off the Moor for a glance at the Kingsbridge Branch and call in at Gara Bridge. It served a small remote community and was not the busiest of places. 4561 arrives with the 1600 Brent-Kingsbridge. March 1961.

Kingsbridge was built as a through station with the extension to Salcombe in mind. This was never built, the GWR instead instituting one of its earliest Omnibus services. The *Bubble Car* has just arrived, there is a substantial amount of parcels and perishables waiting to be loaded, the station is well kept and looks busy, yet the end would come within a month. The site of the station is now an industrial estate. August 1963.

One need only cast a glance at the rolling stock in the branch platform to confirm this hand-coloured postcard is from the Edwardian era. The view is looking towards Plymouth, it was a scene that hardly changed over the years. The still extant goods shed is to the left; notable is the former broad gauge track converted to standard gauge leading in to it. c.1911 The Dartmoor Trust Archive.

An updated view since the demolition of the signal box in November 1914. The goods shed survives in industrial use out of shot to the left. Other than the background hills there is not much to link the two images, 43301 front and 43321 rear hurry by with 1S25 1225 Plymouth–Glasgow Central. 1 November 2017.

The going away shot of 1S51 was a lucky one, that rare perfect pass. Both trains were running late, to the right 43190 leads 1C77 1006 London Paddington–Penzance, to the left 43321 on the rear of 1S51. 1 November 2017.

It was once such a different scene here; 55 years separate the two images. The physical junctions for the Kingsbridge line were at the Totnes end of the station, the single line branch ran in on the right. Note the fine array of signals, my thanks to Doug Nicholls for use of the picture. August 1962.

The now preserved Class 52 D1010 *Western Campaigner* in charge of 1B65 1330 London Paddington–Penzance nearing the end of the climb up Rattery Bank from Totnes, taking the original alignment and is about to enter the original Marley Tunnel, from which it will emerge for its passage through the Dartmoor National Park. Notice how the up and down main lines split here to allow for the two separate single line bores, the second, the up (left) line bore, opened 14 May 1893 on doubling of the line. I am standing just above the tunnel mouth; one can appreciate just how shallow the tunnel is beneath the terrain. This was due to the landowning Palk Carews objecting to seeing the railway crossing their land; the view must not be spoilt! Such was the power of the gentry. 2 June 1976.

The Palk Carew home at Marley House c.1910. The railway runs a few hundred yards beyond the house behind the trees on the left.
The Dartmoor Trust Archive

Totnes is considered as a gateway to the South Hams, we call in here for this is where the Ashburton Branch connected with the outside world. At the foot of Rattery Bank we see 4588 at the west end of Totnes station in the process of running round its train, a poignant one at that, the last opportunity for locals to traverse the full length of the line to the little town just inside the National Park boundary. 2 October 1971.

4561 poses in the up platform with the Ashburton Goods, behind to the right the Brunel built but never used for its intended purpose Pump House for the failed Atmospheric Railway project, to the left the signal box now in use as a highy recommended café. June 1961.

A view which typifies the 1950s when the Western Region of BR still thought itself as part of the GWR. A pair of ex GWR 4-6-0's, an unidentified Grange piloting an unidentified King calls at Totnes with the 0730 Truro to London Paddington. The Ashburton Branch was not provided with its own bay platform. The track lay out at Totnes was ill equipped to deal with a fussy little train running in to the down platform, which then had to be shunted over to the up platform (on occasion a time consuming exercise to be fitted around the main line schedule) to return from whence it came. To save time and because not all the points involved were fitted with facing point locks, quoting from the summer 1955 time table as a typical example, the first train of the day the 0710 from Ashburton due at 0730 returned at 0744 direct from the down platform, this to get out of the way of the 0715 Plymouth–London Paddington due at 0751 and the 0735 Newton Abbot-Penzance due at 0753. It was advertised to commence from Staverton at 0752 and shown in the working time table as empty stock from Totnes to Staverton. Conversations with former colleagues tell of locals and those in the know at times often travelling on the alleged *empty* stock part of the journey, the Booking Office even issuing tickets for it!! 10 July 1957.

The Ashburton Branch

In the case of Ashburton, we have an example of its railway coming from the wrong place. The Stannary Town looked more to the east for its trade and communications and to Newton Abbot in particular. A railway from the latter was the obvious choice and this was the original proposal. It would have required considerable engineering works to overcome the hilly ground between the two, and the money and the backing was not forthcoming. Two miles to the west of Ashburton lay Buckfastleigh; both towns had lost much in trade since the main line from to Plymouth was completed in 1848. Both were associated with the wool trade which had survived the decline in fortunes; Buckfastleigh had kept most of its woollen mills and actually outgrew Ashburton in their number. History: The Buckfastleigh, Totnes and South Devon Railway had its Act passed by Parliament on 25 July 1863; that for the two mile extension to Ashburton received assent on 26 May 1865. Buckfastleigh was the spur for the railway to be built, Ashburton had the money. Thereafter matters did not progress very swiftly. It was on 1 May 1872 that the 9 miles and 20 chains Broad Gauge line linking Totnes and Ashburton, with intermediate stations at Staverton and Buckfastleigh, was opened. The line was worked by the South Devon Railway, with the GWR taking over operations in 1876, converting to standard gauge in May 1892. The broad gauge branch engine marked its passing by arriving at Swindon draped in black crepe presented by the Portreeve of Ashburton. The Buckfastleigh Company (which also owned the Totnes Quay Branch) was taken over by the GWR as from 28 August 1897. After nationalisation in January 1948, BR ran the passenger service for a decade, withdrawal taking effect as from 5 November 1958. The line lingered on for goods until 4555 worked the last freight train from Ashburton on Friday 7 September 1962. The following day 4567 ran a farewell special organised by the Plymouth Railway Circle composed of goods brake vans marking the total closure of the route. But that, it is pleasing to say, is not the end of the story, for most of the line was saved for preservation. The Dart Valley Railway Company took over ownership of the line in October 1965 and a Light Railway Order for its operation by the new owners was granted. Due to various problems it was not until 5 April 1969 passenger servies were restored between Buckfastleigh and a run-round loop named Totnes Riverside, just short of the main line. On 21 May 1969 the infamous Doctor Beeching performed the opening ceremony, commenting: 'If I had not closed this branch, I could not now reopen it'. An error of the first order as the line was not a Beeching closure; it had closed in September 1962, and Beeching did not take up his appointment as Chairman of British Rail until 1 January 1963. Sadly the Buckfastleigh–Ashburton line was not allowed to fully reopen, being used only for the odd enthusiasts' special and for locomotive and stock storage/maintenance at Ashburton. Much of the track bed between Buckfastleigh and Ashburton was earmarked by the Ministry of Transport for being taken over for improvements to the A38 main road. A public enquiry was held and Devon County Council which had opposed the closure of the line in 1958 now opposed its reopening! The final trains ran between Buckfastleigh and Ashburton – the last two coming from Swansea and London Paddington – ran on 2 October 1971, and since then this section has been mostly lost under the A38 dual carriageway. The preserved railway is now run under the aegis of the South Devon Railway Trust from its own Totnes Riverside Station, on which work started in 1977. It runs to a much changed Buckfastleigh and has gone from strength to strength. It is without doubt one of the country's leading heritage railways.

One of the more famed rivers that flow off the moor is the one from which it takes it very name. The East and West Dart converge at Dartmeet, the GWR main line crossing the river at Totnes almost at its tidal limit. From behind D1039 Western King on 1A71 1630 Plymouth-Paddington the view looking towards Ashburton Junction. 28 April 1971.

Four decades later and I lean out of the window again crossing the Dart Viaduct, this time behind Class 43 HST Power Car 43148 on 1A91 1600 Plymouth-Paddington. The view is still recognisable, the most notable difference being the suspension bridge built to carry the footpath opened in 1993 linking the Heritage Railway Station (the view of which is blocked by the growth) with that of the main line. 14 April 2014.

For almost the length of the present day Heritage Railway, the line hugs the east bank of the River Dart, 1450 propelling W228 at Dartington Hall with the 1547 Totnes-Buckfastleigh. A grubby 14XX engine so synonymous to the branch and maroon auto coach, pure nostalgia. 18 February 2013.

A mirror image reflection of Collett 0-6-0 3205passing with the 1500 Totnes-Buckfastleigh; tender engines were unknown on the line in the pre preservation era. 16 February 2017.

The view from near Five Lanes Cross in the early Heritage Railway era. Buckfastleigh station is mostly hidden by the trees, the former station master's house stands out. Behind is the then single-carriageway A38 road. Looking in the distance the houses nestling in the valley are the south end of Buckfastleigh with to the top left Brent Hill. October 1970.

Same field almost half a century later, the changes are extraordinary. The most obvious are of Buckfastleigh station and its yard. The engineering works now occupies the space between the River Dart and the station with to the right the carriage shed completed in late 2017. The other standout feature is the dual carriageway A38 on a new alignment constructed 1971–72. 8 March 2018.

From the A384 Totnes road bridge, 4588 slows for the approach to Buckfastleigh with 1Z45 1505 Ashburton-London Paddington, the very last train from the moorland terminus. 2 October 1971.

The updated view is taken from the much larger overpass at the A38/A384 junction, the changes are dramatic and speak for themselves, and the background hill confirms the location. 31 August 2014.

The Branch passed under the A38 at Pear Tree where it entered the National Park. From the old road on the outskirts of Ashburton, 6435+1638 head the last train bound for the Moorland Terminus 1Z45 0825 London Paddington–Ashburton heading away from Gulwell Tunnel, the eastern portal hidden by the tree-lined cutting. 2 October 1971.

This updated view is taken at a slightly lower level but there is a common link between the two images. In the upper photograph two people can just be seen standing in the top left of the field and there is a small ridge, that same little ridge is the one in the top left of the bank in this view. 8 March 2018.

Standing in that same field, we turn the other way to witness 4588 pulling away from Ashburton with the last train of all to depart from the station, 1Z45 1505 Ashburton–London Paddington. 2 October 1971.

Again taken at a slightly lower angle, the arc of the trees follows the curve of the former railway. To help link the two pictures, to the left behind the trees one can just spot a house and in the original view it is just above the cab of 4588. 8 March 2018.

Opposite top: Weeds have taken over on the approach to Ashburton station. To the left the premises of Edwin Tucker & Sons, Maltsters and Seed Merchants remind us of the time when the railways were the life-blood of many an agricultural community. Tuckers was established in 1831 and, due to changing markets, closed on 22 December 2018. To the right is the small engine shed and, distant, alongside the goods shed, is the station with its Brunel wooden overall roof. 20 June 1965.

Opposite lower: Livestock, cattle in particular, was very much a feature of traffic forwarded from Ashburton, this persisting until the end of the line. Just three months before closure Class 03 D2130 is a rare visitor, ready to leave with an outgoing lengthy cattle special. Diesels were almost unknown on the line in the BR era. Behind the train the rather cramped terminus, the goods shed to the left. The station lay very close to the centre of the town. Immediately behind it stood a local landmark, the spire of the Parish Church of St Andrew with its four clock faces. 7 June 1962.

Below: The scene at present. This could soon change as proposals for development are in the air. It is believed there will no building on any former railway land, and the footpath on the former track bed leading back to Pear Tree will be protected. It leaves that cherished hope that Ashburton could once again be connected by the railway, but it would be expensive. The station is now a garage, the view of the wooden overall roof obscured by building alterations. The goods shed survives, and it is listed and now in commercial use. St Andrew's church still keeps watch over the station. 30 August 2014.

To seek our next railway which penetrated Dartmoor, we have moved east from Totnes 8½ miles to Newton Abbot – still the junction for passengers travelling to Torbay. Here one once changed for the Moretonhampstead Branch. The view below and that on the opposite page are taken from the same window in South Devon House half a century apart. Of particular note in the older photograph is the platform to the far left with its commanding water tower, this is number 9, the Moretonhampstead branch platform, keeping its trains clear of the main line. Immediately behind is Tuckers Maltings with the power station beyond dominating the scene. Standing against the green of the racecourse is East Signal Box where D1054 Western Governor has collected the Kingswear portion and is about to reverse back with it to attach to 1A84 1200 Penzance-London Paddington waiting on Platform 6. On the up through line D600 awaits with an east bound freight train, opposite reading from left to right are Platforms 7 and 5, with numbers 3 and 1 on the opposite (down side) island; the west end of the same islands carried even numbered platforms. To the right of the latter the lines leading to and from Hackney Yard lay alongside extensive carriage sidings crammed full of stock. Newton Abbot was back then a major railway centre. June 1965.

Newton Abbot GWR station building, opened in 1927. Now known as South Devon House, the building has altered little in appearance.

The Dartmoor Trust Archive

The changes are many and drastic – as the comparative photograph belows shows. The power station was demolished in the spring of 1975 and the track layout severely rationalised in May 1987 when the signal boxes closed and the area passed to the control of the Exeter Panel Signal Box. The surviving platforms from right to left become numbers 1, 2 and 3 for their whole length. Amazingly Platform 9 still retains its track and in fairly recent times has been used for loco-motive stabling purposes. Tuckers Maltings at the time still provided for the brewing industry. 143 619 arrives with 2T14 1249 Exeter St Davids–Paignton; note to its left the still extant connection to what is now the Heathfield and was once the Moretonhampstead Branch. Sadly Tuckers Maltings, one of only four malt houses in the country to remain providing malt in the traditional manner, closed after 187 years of production at the end of October 2018. 10 September 2015.

The Moretonhampstead Branch

Moretonhampstead, the eastern gateway to Dartmoor; it is just over twelve miles from Newton Abbot with a climb of 550 feet. Like so many rural branch lines it was built by a local company which found itself short of the necessary financial backing, delaying construction. Poor weather also intervened, particularly the unprecedented winter of 1865. The climb from the head of the estuary of the River Teign to the high moor was fairly gradual and there were no major engineering works.

History: A section of the former Haytor Granite Tramway was used by the Moretonhampstead & South Devon Railway who opened their 7'–¼ broad gauge line of 12 miles and 28 chains on 4 July 1866 from Newton Abbot to Moretonhampstead, with intermediate stations at Bovey Tracey and Lustleigh. Teigngrace station between Newton Abbot and Chudleigh Road was opened 16 December 1867 at the insistence of the Lord of the Manor of Stover. The company always had financial woes and sought amalgamation with the South Devon Railway which took place with effect from 1 July 1872. The SDR would only be owners of the line for a brief period as they themselves were absorbed by the GWR on 1 February 1876, with formal amalgamation of the two companies taking place on 1 August 1878.

There had since day one been calls for a station near Jew's Bridge, and this was provided from 1 July 1874, named Chudleigh Road, this changing to Heathfield from 2 October 1882. Seven days later Heathfield became a junction with the opening of the standard gauge Teign Valley line to Ashton, more of which anon. The Moretonhampstead branch was converted from broad to standard gauge over the weekend of 20-22 May 1892, removing the need for the physical transhipment of goods between the two railways at Heathfield when through working became possible. A junction between the two lines facing Moretonhampstead but through a siding came during the following year. Two further stations were added in an attempt to attract local custom. The first, Brimley Halt, on the southern outskirts of Bovey Tracey opened on 21 May 1928 and Hawkmoor Halt between Bovey Tracey and Lustleigh followed on 1 June 1931. Built to attract walkers to the moor, and also to serve Hawkmoor Hospital, the drawback was that the latter, a sanatorium for tuberculosis, was two miles away along winding country lanes which many a visitor found out the hard way! The little station was renamed Pullabrook Halt as from 13 June 1955 – one would suspect to due to the number of complaints which no doubt ensued – and sadly Pullabrook Halt would have a short life.

The passenger service between Newton Abbot and Moretonhampstead was withdrawn as from 2 March 1959. Goods facilities were withdrawn from Lustleigh and Moretonhampstead as from 6 April 1964, with total closure of the line beyond Bovey Tracey – the track on this section being recovered in the spring/summer of 1965. Next to go was Bovey Tracey, closing completely after the loss of the grain traffic to the road hauliers. The complete closure of Heathfield–Bovey was marked on Sunday 5 July 1970 when four special trains were run by BR from Platform 9 at Newton Abbot to Bovey Tracey and return. The track was ripped up beyond the

4¾ mile post with indecent haste and gone by 8 September the same year. Newton Abbot–Heathfield remained open in fits and starts for freight varying from bananas and Candy's tiles, the oil depot at Heathfield and china clay. The collapse of the EWS Speedlink freight network in July 1991 spelt the end of the ball clay traffic at Kingsteignton and from Heathfield the following year. The oil traffic at Heathfield ended with the arrival of the last train behind 37 896 on 20 December 1995. Except for the odd rail tour, the line lay dormant until a weekly clay train was restarted from Heathfield by EWS in May 1998 and ran until December 2006. After another dormant period the line was mothballed with closure thought to be inevitable. However, this was a line that refused to die and it gained a further lease of life when bulk timber was loaded from Teign Bridge to Chirk in North Wales starting 7 December 2011, the empty incoming train having to go to Heathfield for the engine to run round. This traffic ceased in April 2015 when it was transferred to Exeter Riverside since when the line has again been mothballed. At the time of writing its future is very uncertain, the track quietly rusting away. There exists a group to reopen the line as a park and ride facility for Newton Abbot and doubtless it would make an attractive heritage railway, but is there room for another one with the Kingswear and Ashburton lines in the vicinity? Network Rail the current owners are in no hurry to dispose of the track, giving interested parties an opportunity to come up with a realistic plan for reopening. We can only wait and see.

Seen from the Kingsteignton road bridge a three-car DMU passes by with 1Z64 1825 Heathfield to Bristol Temple Meads rail tour. To the left are the still waters of River Teign, to the right the goods shed which by this time had become a rail served depot for National Carriers. 20 April 1974.

That peaceful riverside scene on the previous page could be on another planet. Look to the right and the chimney of the former goods shed provides a link between the pictures. A rare visitor to the line, a High Speed Train, passes slowly through the present day jungle. 43187 leads with 43188 on the rear with 1Z67 1125 Buckfastleigh- Heathfield. 10 October 2015.

1½ miles from Newton Abbot lay Teignbridge Crossing, a last day special from Bovey Tracey about to pass the former crossing keeper's house, from September 1947 used purely as a crossing keeper's cabin. After the cessation of passenger services the crossing was converted for operation by train crews. This original piece of the branch infrastructure is Grade II listed. In the foreground are the sidings used for the ball clay traffic, taken out of use in 1988 as far as I know. 5 July 1970.

37 019 with 6C58 1045 Heathfield-St Blazey, formed of two of the larger Tiger air braked wagons introduced in 1982. A member of the train crew has closed the gates after the passage of the convoy over the road. This traffic would cease within a couple of years. Notice how the sidings here are now showing signs of neglect. 4 April 1990.

Heathfield, where the branch runs along the course of the former Hay Tor Granite Tramway; the view from the A38 road bridge looking towards Moretonhampstead as a last day special from Bovey calls. Regular passenger trains had not run through here for over a decade, yet the station still had the appearance of being a country railway junction. The former Candy & Co siding is the one to the immediate left. The DMU stands at the former up platform with the former bay for Teign Valley trains behind, the latter now occupied by goods wagons serving the still healthy and varied traffic which existed here at the time. At the rear of the train the former Teign Valley line can be seen curving away to the right from its double line junction with the Moretonhampstead line, although by this time only a small portion survived for head shunt purposes. 5 July 1970.

Above: The view from the A38 at Heathfield station has changed much over the years, 150 234 waiting to depart on the shortest day of the year with 2Z53 1250 Heathfield–Newton Abbot. I think it best for the changes to speak for themselves. 21 December 2014.

Heathfield station and the Candy tile works c.1920.
The Dartmoor Trust Archive

D857 *Undaunted* taking the former Teign Valley route with an engineering train, a short section of the route here retained as access to the bay platform and the Geest warehouse was only possible by reversal from this line. 3 October 1971.

The Teign Valley Branch is, strictly speaking, beyond the terms of reference for this volume as it did not enter Dartmoor. However, it started from a railway bound for the moor and at its western end had a couple of stations which served a village and a town, both gateways to Dartmoor. The history of the route is remarkable for the number of Acts of Parliament to coax it into life. From its first Act it took fifty years and two separate companies to complete the always-single line standard gauge branch. The first company, the Teign Valley, needed nine Acts to come into existence and another three afterwards, which must be a record for a 7¾ mile railway. The first part to open was from Heathfield to Ashton on 9 October 1882, and soon after another mile for goods. The Exeter Railway completed the link over the hills when Ashton to Exeter City Basin Junction opened on 1 July 1903. The whole route was worked as one unit and was always known as the Teign Valley Branch. Passenger traffic was never heavy and the mineral traffic from the Teign Valley mines had gradually waned. Passenger services were withdrawn as from 9 June 1958, Alphington–Christow closing completely. Goods continued from Heathfield to Christow until the line was damaged by flooding between Trusham and Ashton in September 1960. With the cessation of traffic from Trusham Cement Works the last goods train ran on 4 December 1967, formal closure announced in July 1968. The track bed between Chudleigh Knighton and Chudleigh is now buried under the A38 dual carriageway. Much else of the route has been lost although there is, as we shall see, activity at Christow.

Chudleigh Knighton Halt looking towards Exeter was opened 9 June 1924 and its level crossing was 1½ miles from Heathfield. It served local needs and the odd hiker seeking a different path up on to the moor. The crossing keeper's cottage survives but sadly due to growth an updated view is impossible. 20 June 1965.

Chudleigh station looking towards Exeter. The town, a gateway to the eastern moor, lies half a mile away up a steep hill. It was a simple station of wooden buildings with a spacious goods yard. The over bridge bears the then A38 road. Today this view is completely lost under the aptly named Chudleigh Station interchange of the A38. 25 June 1965.

Moving on up the line by a couple of stations before returning to the Moreton-hampstead branch, we make a brief visit to Christow where the railway actually leaves the Teign Valley. In effect, the river valley on to the moor turns left, the railway to pass over, and in two instances under, the hills to Exeter. Unlike the quarried granite of Dartmoor which can be cut and shaped, the eastern edge of the moor along the Teign Valley comprised a black hard form of igneous rock known as basalt. This can be crushed and graded into hardwearing road stone, aggregate and ballast. It was only after the arrival of the railway in 1882 that these reserves could be exploited as the means to transport them away now existed.

One of the later basalt quarries to open was Scatter Rock in 1914, connected to a new siding at Christow station by an aerial ropeway system with forty circulating half ton skips which carried the stone direct from the quarry to the rail head. It is this we see passing above the Teign House Inn at Christow in this picture from the Dartmoor Trust Archive. The group gathered are members of the Cheriton Hunt who, no doubt, would have enjoyed partaking in The City Brewery Ales & Stouts on offer. Happily this much recommended establishment is still going strong. The City Brewery referred to is the Exeter City Brewery, taken over by Whitbread in 1967 when brewing was transferred to Tiverton with their Exeter premises demolished in the early 1970s as part of the construction of the Exe Road Bridge system. It appears the aerial ropeway was taken out of use around 1929 and no trace of it remains today. The quarry is deserted and flooded but there is activity in the area where the former ropeway met the railway. 1923.

A project to bring Christow goods yard back to life started in 1984, best described as a private museum open occasionally in the summer months, and by request. For further details see www.teignrail.co.uk. The scene is in the former Scatter Rock Siding where the aerial ropeway once terminated with Perseus, relics of the past and a selection of varied rolling stock of various gauges. 17 June 2000.

Pottery Bridge took the A382 over the Moretonhampstead branch, a graceful double-arch structure of limestone with brick spiral arches, demolished in 1986 amid much protest to make room for the Bovey bypass. Behind me was the former granite siding where the line left the route of the Haytor Granite Tramway. 25 June 1965.

The Haytor Granite Tramway

Having been following for the last couple of miles or so what was originally the course of the Haytor Granite Tramway, this is therefore a very convenient point to briefly leave the Moretonhampstead branch to follow the Tramway to the High Moor. It was one of the first and surely the most unique of the railways which penetrated Dartmoor. Passengers were never carried; this was purely a railway for granite.

In the early years of the nineteenth century, good quality granite was in demand, and the area around Haytor had a very good supply of it. Transporting it over what were then very primitive roads was a problem; the logical outlet was to the River Teign and onward by coastal shipping. The Stover Canal had been built by James II Templer to aid the transport of ball clay to the River Teign at Hackney (in modern day terms between Newton Abbot Race Course and the main GWR line) from Ventiford, opening in 1792. It was extended in 1820 to Teigngrace where it then acted as a feeder for traffic from the 10 mile-long Haytor Granite Tramway. The latter was built without an Act of Parliament, opening with much local celebration on 16 September 1820 and can be considered as the first railway of any sort not only on Dartmoor but in Devon as a whole. Instead of iron rails hewn blocks formed the flanged rails, varying from four to eight feet in length, built to a gauge of 4 feet 3 inches. The wheels of the iron wagons were flangeless.

The line was certainly an early candidate for notable civil engineering; it descended the better part of 1300 feet following the contours from the High Moor to meet the Teign, it was constructed to follow a consistent downward gradient allowing gravity to propel the loaded wagons downhill while horsepower brought empty wagons back to the quarry. The cost of the granite was high, it had to be transferred from the tramway to canal barges at Teigngrace, and then at Teignmouth from the barges to coastal shipping. For a while the demand was high but cheaper granite came on the market and in 1858 the tramway fell in to disuse, although the quarries remained active into the 1880s.

There was, in 1905, a scheme to electrify the line in order to run a service of trams. This failed to materialise and in retrospect it was the correct outcome for the whole character of the line and the area would have changed for the worst. Little remains of the tramway at its southern end. Beyond the site of Granite Siding as the track bed climbs up to the Moor, sections survive in the area of Yarner Wood.

The best place to see it is in the area of Haytor itself. The whole area around and including the Tor, the quarries and the granite rails of the Tramway are protected from development and disturbance and are a site of Special Scientific Interest. The rails are listed as a National Monument. There are no known photographs of the Tramway in its working era although early prints show the quarries and tramway in operation.

Looking across what would have been the level crossing with the Manaton Road, the view is looking south east down the grade through Haytor Vale towards Teigngrace. The gradual descent following the contours is noticeable if the eye follows the track bed across the road past the small hedge to left and then curving away to the right beyond the wind battered tree. 31 August 2014.

Extensive activity at Haytor from an 1829 print. Lower centre a horse can be seen drawing a wagon away from the quarry loaded with a massive granite block.
The Dartmoor Trust Archive

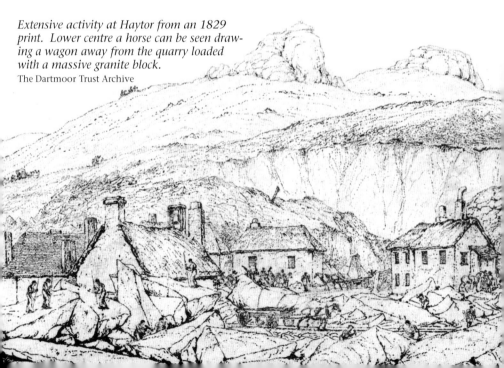

Looking up towards the Manaton Road with what is probably the remains of a crossing loop, the unique track, its point-work and the gradual gradient of the route all clearly evident. To the top left of the picture stands the outcrop which is Hay Tor itself. 31 August 2014.

This is a railway junction like no other, that of the quarry to the right and Saddle Tor lines to the left, the granite rails and point-work perfectly preserved. When points were encountered, the wheels of the wagons were guided by point tongues pivoted on the granite blocks rails, it is not known if these were made of iron or oak. 31 August 2014.

As fine a curve as one would find on many a country and mineral railway, but this one is made of granite taking the line in to the quarry by the tor which is behind the photographer. The straight line onwards towards Saddle Tor and Holwell can clearly be picked out behind. 31 August 2014.

Opposite top: Bovey Tracey is also a gateway to Dartmoor. Its station – appearing in the time tables simply as 'Bovey' was very convenient for the town. The view is from the level crossing looking towards Moretonhampstead. The main station buildings were sited on the up platform to the right, nestling behind a round topped corrugated iron store; this started its life as a bus waiting shelter, more of which below. 20 June 1965.

Opposite bottom: The Bovey bypass opened in 1987 was driven on the track bed through the former station. The iron hut where day trippers once took shelter was acquired by the South Devon Railway in 1985, and is now in use as the stores hut at Totnes Riverside station. The station buildings survive as the Bovey Heritage Centre office and archive room. The goods shed beyond is now occupied by the Dartmoor National Park Association as their maintenance depot. In between is a standard GWR Toad goods brake van number 114906, built in 1928 and acquired by the Bovey Heritage Trust in 2010. 30 August 2014.

The GWR were early pioneers in the development of road motor transport, establishing a network of routes and their own vehicles to operate them. Their peak can be said to be the post First World War era. Here, c.1925, outside Bovey station, the GWR-owned charabancs await the train to take the tourists to the moor. In the foreground to the right is XY 2110 its destination board showing 'Bovey, Becky Falls & Manaton', and to its left T 7692 is bound for 'Haytor Rocks', these being the most popular destinations. The unidentified charabanc immediately behind T7692 displays the legend 'Princetown' – at 17½ miles the longest run from here, and a taxing one at that for these early vehicles. Parked up outside the bus waiting shelter, fulfilling its original use, is L 6307. To the right of the goods shed, the back siding, only accessible from Newton Abbot by reversal, appears to contain its maximum capacity of 28 wagons. The Dartmoor Trust Archive.

Opposite: A busy scene at Lustleigh, recorded by my good friend Alistair Jeffery, but sadly a one-off as the station had closed to passengers 3½ years earlier. This is the second of two rail tours run by the then South Devon Railway Society to Moretonhampstead conveying over 200 passengers from Paignton. Although the tour was a success, the Society hoped this would stimulate BR in to revisiting the possibility of restoring the branch passenger service as DMU's were now well established in the area. This was a lost cause, as was their aspiration to run the line themselves, which at the time was still open for freight. Attention turned to the Ashburton Branch and the rest, as they say, is history. Lustleigh is one of Dartmoor's most charming villages and in its day it had a railway station to match. The flags are out at Lustleigh for Large Prairie 5153 and its train, the platform jammed full of people with a period selection of cars parked up as the locals gather to witness the display. Such numbers a decade earlier on a daily basis may well have meant a turn in fortune for the railway. An attempt to update the view from the road bridge proved meaningless due to the substantial foliage blocking the scene. The station remains as a private residence. 11 June 1962.

Lustleigh station was temporarily renamed Baskerville Halt for the making of the first sound version film, released in 1931, and also the first to use actual Dartmoor locations for *The Hound of the Baskervilles* . Photographic trickery is nothing new. In the film Sherlock Holmes is seen travelling on the alleged Paddington express with a distant view of the train rounding curves at Kings Tor on the Princetown Branch, only seconds later miraculously to alight at Baskerville! Distance as the crow flies 17 miles, the journey by train 64 miles. The Dartmoor Trust Archive.

Wray Barton is where rail, road and the Wray stream came together, a rural setting within the National Park. Passing with the thrice-weekly goods to Moretonhampstead 9768 has a payload of one grain and one coal wagon. 12 August 1961.

The course of the former line is clearly visible; the Wray is to the right where it passes under the former branch. To the extreme left the hedge marks a bend in the A382. 8 March 2018.

9768 has arrived at Moretonhampstead and stopped outside the engine shed, a broad gauge specimen built with the opening of the station. Due to the condition of the structure, it was closed in1947. In true BR style, having closed the shed due to its precarious state, they repaired it in 1949 and the Co-op leased it as a coal store. 12 August 1961.

The station and its yard are now occupied by Thompsons Road Haulage, with few reminders of the railway terminus which once existed here. There are plans to develop the site with housing. One building to survive intact is the broad gauge engine shed, now in use as a store, and is a listed structure. 8 March 2018.

Moretonhampstead engine shed is a solid granite structure of 43 feet by 22 feet. The Thompson Haulage staff were very welcoming and access was kindly granted into the building, still with an atmosphere all of its own. Look carefully and some rails can still be seen lying on the floor, The granite walls show up well in this interior view well lit by the day light entering through the four windows on each side. 8 March 2018.

Continuing the broad gauge theme here a gem from the Dartmoor Archive, not of the best quality, but pictures of that era are rare. It provides good detail of the train shed of its architecture and construction. A member of the station staff poses for the undated picture, taken shortly prior to the gauge conversion of 1892.

From the branch passenger train in its early days to how it looked in its final days as 4179 waits to leave with the 1015 to Newton Abbot. The view is taken further back from the lower picture on the previous page and gives us a good view of the granite built goods shed with its sturdy doors. 15 February 1958.

Moretonhampstead – the name for the town comes from the old English for a farmstead in the moorland – is the gateway to North East Dartmoor, and it was reputed to be the longest single name station board name on the GWR; incidentally Buckfastleigh is the longest where none of the letters of the alphabet repeat themselves. 20 June 1965.

The extension of the line the 4½ miles to Chagford never materialised. A horse-drawn coach began around 14 April 1868 running at first on Tuesdays and Fridays. It was certainly running daily by 1889 and supported by the GWR as we see above in this c.1890 picture from the Dartmoor Trust Archive outside the Globe Hotel at Chagford. Road motors were introduced by the GWR on the route in 1906, a year later than intended due to a dispute with the County Council over who would pay for the road improvements necessary. That was not the first bus service to reach Chagford. The LSWR had started a direct service from Exeter Queen Street (now Central) 1 June 1904. One assumes the comfort of their passengers was not a consideration! This is of note as between 1905 and 1908 the two vehicles employed were Clarksons steam buses. It would be interesting to know how these managed to cope with the sub standard roads and the hills. As both the roads and the buses improved the LSWR faced some stiff competition until throwing in the towel at the end of September 1924.

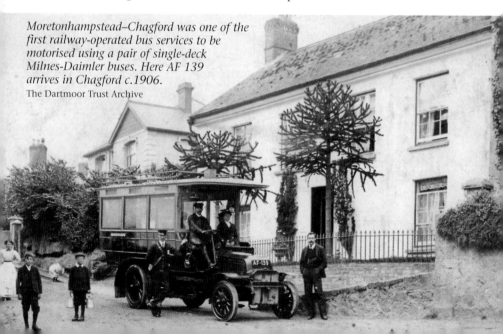

Moretonhampstead–Chagford was one of the first railway-operated bus services to be motorised using a pair of single-deck Milnes-Daimler buses. Here AF 139 arrives in Chagford c.1906.
The Dartmoor Trust Archive

Having completed the first part of our circular tour by rail of Dartmoor from Ivybridge, it is now time to move from the Southern Moor to the Northern Moor. By train the logical route from Moretonhampstead to Okehampton would be via Exeter. Using the 1955 time table, Moretonhampstead depart 1015, Newton Abbot arrive 1050, depart 1110. Exeter St Davids arrive 1136 and then changing to the green railway, depart 1154 to arrive at Okehampton at 1253, a total distance of 58½ miles with a journey time of just over 2½ hours. Or we could catch a bus; it is 14.6 miles from Moretonhampstead to Okehampton by road via the A382/A30, a perfect example of how the railways went around Dartmoor as opposed to going through it.

In a scene which could have been taken in the 1950s, Carmel Coaches Albion Victor with a Duple Body registration LOD 495 dating from 1950 stands outside Okehampton Station having worked the 174 service over the Moor from Moretonhampstead. This service was part of the Dartmoor Sunday Rover ticket, introduced in the early 1990s by the County Council to stimulate access by public transport to Dartmoor. This was at the time when the Sunday Rover was at its height with a network of bus services radiating across Dartmoor. As Government funding for Local Government has been reduced in recent years, subsides for the Sunday Dartmoor bus network were a casualty and sadly they are now almost non existent. 3 June 2001.

Also awaiting custom from the last train of the day from Exeter is Bristol Lodekka 824 KDV, resplendent in its green Western National livery. It is working the number 118 to Plymouth routed via Gunnislake. Here passengers had the option to complete their journey by train using the other principal Dartmoor Sunday Rover train service between Gunnislake and Plymouth, fulfilling that missing link in the rails. With the Carmel Coach behind, it presents a perfect example of rail–road integrated transport where each connected with the other, and these Sunday Rover inter-connecting routes were popular and well used. Over the years the Sunday trains between Exeter and Okehampton have been reduced from six to four. Is there a wasted opportunity here to take people out of their cars on to the moor perhaps? After an absence of many years, the Sunday Gunnislake Station-Okehampton Station Sunday bus service was reintroduced for the 2019 season, operated by Plymouth City Bus with a new route number 279. A step in the right direction one feels. 3 June 2001.

The Southern Railway main line Exeter–Plymouth

Of the three main communicating routes built between Exeter and Plymouth, this was the longest. The distance between the two cities by the railway via Okehampton was 58½ miles, by the surviving rail route through Dawlish it is 52 miles, and the distance by road between Exeter St Davids and Plymouth Station via the A38 is 45 miles. It is the part between Sampford Courtenay and Tavistock which is of relevance to this volume, in particular travelling from east to west the course of the line runs through the National Park from a point mid way between Okehampton and Meldon where it passes beneath the A30 road, the northern boundary of the National Park at this point, leaving it just to the east of Tavistock. The LSWR route did not project any branch lines in to the Moor.

History: Its construction was piecemeal. To cut a long and complex story very short, the North Devon Railway extended the line from Crediton to Barnstaple opening on 12 July 1854, becoming LSWR property 1 January 1865. The Okehampton Railway was authorised to build a line from Coleford 4½ miles to the west of Crediton. By the time it opened it had become the Devon & Cornwall Railway, being taken over by the LSWR. Coleford Junction–North Tawton opened on 1 November 1865, North Tawton–Okehampton Road (the present day Sampford Courtenay) on 8 January 1867, Okehampton Road–Okehampton on 3 October 1871 and Okehampton–Lidford on 12 October 1874. Here the Devon & Cornwall Station was built alongside that of the GWR Plymouth–Launceston branch, which had arrived here in 1865. Much to the chagrin of the LSWR the onward traffic to Tavistock and Plymouth went forward on the GWR; goods between the systems had to be transhipped by hand due to the differing gauges.

The Plymouth–Tavistock section of the branch had been built by the South Devon & Tavistock, the extension to Launceston by the Launceston & South Devon. Under the terms of the Act of Parliament for the latter, the Board of Trade had the power to order laying of standard gauge rails and that running powers be granted to any connecting company. A similar power had been imposed on the South Devon & Tavistock in 1854. The Devon & Cornwall took up the option, after a dispute with the broad gauge companies, and made an attempt to build an independent route more or less parallel with the GWR branch down to Marsh Mills. The South Devon Railway which by now owned both companies was obliged to lay a third rail on the section to Plymouth with further works in the Plymouth area.

The arrangements came into operation when the LSWR began running over the line from Lidford and into its own Devonport terminal on 18 May 1876. Tavistock welcomed the LSWR with more enthusiasm than it did when the broad gauge had come to the town in June 1859, a point not lost of the Directors of the GWR. The LSWR was limited in the number of trains it could run over the branch, priority was invariably given to the GWR, and the layout and workings of the mixed gauge line, especially at the crossing stations on the route, are best described as complicated and cumbersome.

The LSWR were swift to improve their main line to Lidford which was originally built as single track with sections doubled progressively from 1877. In 1879 Okehampton (Meldon) became a junction station for the branch to Halwill and, eventually, to Bude and Padstow.

It was the Plymouth Devonport & South Western Junction Railway that built the independent route from Lidford to Devonport by way of the Tamar Valley, entering Plymouth along the eastern bank of the River Tamar, with substantial engineering works between St Budeaux and Devonport, its double track main line opening on 2 June 1890. The former LSWR terminus at Devonport was altered to become a through station as the trains worked through to Plymouth North Road. Surprisingly the LSWR did not take up the option to purchase this independent concern, but did take full responsibility for the route for which the PDSWJR were paid a very good dividend. The stations were painted in the LSWR colours, staffed by their personnel and LSWR boundary markers marked its line-side limits. The story of Plymouth's Railways and the rivalry there between the GWR and the LSWR is covered in the author's books *Backtracking Around Friary, Laira and the Plym*, and *Backtracking Around Millbay, Saltash and the Tamar*.

At the Grouping in 1923, the LSWR and the PDSWJR were both absorbed into the Southern Railway. On nationalisation in 1948, all the former Southern Railway routes west of Exeter passed to the Southern Region of British Railways. From 1952 to 1958 commercial responsibility for the SR routes passed to the Western Region although the Southern continued to operate it. As from 1 January 1963, on the same day that Dr Richard Beeching took up his position as Chairman of the British Railways Board, all former SR lines west of Wilton South were transferred to the Western Region. This would be the start of five years of great change for the SR route via Okehampton.

Below: The winds of change are blowing at Okehampton; rebuilt *Battle of Britain* Class 34062 *17 Squadron* pauses with the 1300 Waterloo–Plymouth. In the bay platform N Class 31840 awaits with the 1751 to Padstow. Within five years steam and through trains from Waterloo would be a memory, the station would cease to be a junction and revert to being the terminus of a branch from Coleford Junction as the route between here and Bere Alston was severed. Within a decade it would be passengers no more, but there is a twist in that tale. August 1963.

Above: By the time the Millennium dawned, from the despair of run-down and closure the restored station was reopened, although on a much reduced scale to the halcyon days of the past. On summer Sundays connections could also be made to go west, albeit not very far. To the right the 1740 from Meldon formed with vehicles 61743+80225 and Austerity 68006 has arrived to connect with 150 249 in the Up platform with the 1825 to Exeter and Exmouth. 3 June 2001.

Thus Paddington had at long last taken full control of its rival's route. Revenge was brutal. Dramatic changes came as from 7 September 1964 when all through trains, with the exception of the overnight from London Waterloo, the 1653 Plymouth–Eastleigh and the through Brighton each way, were withdrawn. The line was singled between Meldon Quarry and Meldon Junction on 24 April 1966 due to concern over the condition of Meldon Viaduct. The timetable of March 1967 heralded the end of the remaining through trains. Poor connections, especially at Exeter (a couple of trains between Exeter and Plymouth in each direction being routed via Gunnislake and adding 90 minutes to the through journey) only aided the case for closure as passenger numbers decreased due to the deliberately poor service provided. From 6 May 1968 the passenger service between Okehampton and Bere Alston was withdrawn, with Okehampton–Meldon Quarry being retained only for freight, otherwise closure was total. St Budeaux–Bere Alston was incorporated in what was now the Gunnislake Branch. Further rationalisation occurred as from 22 March 1970 when Okehampton–Meldon Quarry was singled, followed by that of Crediton–Okehampton as from 17 October 1971. Coleford Junction was abolished, the now singled Barnstaple and Okehampton lines running as parallel tracks over what was the up and down main line until they just now simply turn away from each other.

Exeter–Okehampton was not listed for closure in the Beeching Report of 1963 and the intention of keeping Okehampton as the railhead for North Cornwall in particular was commendable. However, people taking the bus from Bude, for example, just stayed on the vehicle until it reached Exeter and use of what was still a reasonable service continued to decline, the passenger service being withdrawn between Exeter and Okehampton as from 5 June 1972.

Okehampton signal box closed 10 July 1972, leaving Crediton–Meldon Quarry in effect as a long mineral siding. Some goods traffic was handled at Okehampton until February 1981; thereafter the line continued its somewhat obscure existence with up to five trains a day transporting quarried stone. In March 1994 Meldon Quarry was sold by BR to ECC Quarries Ltd; later the same year this became Camas Aggregates PLC and is now part of Bardon Aggregates. The deal included the railway line to a point immediately before the former Coleford Junction along with Meldon Viaduct and Okehampton Station (the latter had seen occasional use since the 1972 closure).

The new owners of the route were keen to support regeneration and a plan developed involving Devon County Council, West Devon Borough Council and Dartmoor National Park to restore Okehampton station to enhance tourism. In 1996 the County Council purchased it for a nominal £1 and on 24 May 1997, superbly restored in its Southern Railway livery, the station was reopened. The following week a Sundays-only seasonal service running May to September between Exeter and Okehampton, calling also at Crediton (Sampford Courtenay was added for the 2008 season), was inaugurated and has run ever since.

The Dartmoor Railway is a unique partnership between Aggregate Industries, RMS Locotec, Devon County Council, West Devon Borough Council and Dartmoor National Park. This took over the lease and maintenance of the route in 1997, establishing their own heritage services by reopening Okehampton to Meldon as from 21 April 2000. A new station called Meldon Quarry was built on part of the original Meldon Quarry Halt (rebuilt and lengthened in 2002), and renamed Meldon Viaduct in July 2015. It is at present the only station open for passengers within the boundary of the National Park. British American Railway Services Ltd, owned by Iowa Pacific Holdings of Chicago took over the lease of the line on 4 September 2008 with ambitions to restore passenger and freight services to the line. These have yet to come to fruition. The last ballast train from Meldon Quarry ran in July 2009, the quarry mothballed in 2011. So at the time of writing this is the present situation of the former LSWR main line around northern Dartmoor.

The halcyon days of Southern steam over the northern route around the moor are recalled in this evocative view of rebuilt Bulleid Pacific 34016 *Bodmin* heading around the Coleford Curve with the *Devon Quarryman* 1Z96 0724 Alton–Meldon Quarry. The train is about to cross the boundary of the present-day Dartmoor Railway with Network Rail, this is immediately to the Okehampton side of the road bridge just out of camera range to the left of the photographer. The Barnstaple line is behind the train but hidden by the trees. Audrey Mills. 30 September 2000.

To begin our look at the relevant part of the line, we start at Sampford Courtenay A single car DMU departs for Okehampton. By now the Okehampton branch, it still looks like a double track main line. The hills of Dartmoor form a distant backdrop. August 1971.

It is now a much changed scene from the B3215 road bridge. Making its way past the overhanging growth Peak 45 060 *Sherwood Forester* leads with the 1255 Meldon Quarry to the Dartmoor Railway boundary at Coleford Junction, proof indeed that the line is still capable of handling main line trains. 5 February 2017.

34084 *253 Squadron* eases its way around the gentle curve with the rear of the train still on Fatherford Viaduct with the 0803 Surbiton–Okehampton Car Carrier, on time and due at its destination at 1228. 29 August 1964.

To stand in the same position today the photographer would be on the east-bound carriageway of the Okehampton bypass. Opened in 1988, this road now demarks the readjusted northern boundary of the National Park. A layby on the west-bound carriageway gave access to the hill from which this comparison view was taken. The Sprinter is passing where we see the rear of the Car Carrier above. The same photo today would be impossible due to increased growth. 1 June 1997.

Okehampton, like Bovey Tracey, stands close to the border of the National Park but that is where the similarities end. Bovey lies in a basin while Okehampton stands at a much higher elevation – 500 feet above sea level – with the station a futher 200 feet above the town. From the Dartmoor Archive comes this Victorian view of Okehampton Station looking towards Meldon, with staff and passengers posing for the camera. c.1890.

Okehampton Station restored in 1997; one can feel the air and space under that canopy and admire the brickwork of the station building. Looking as though it may have come from Tavistock, 150 249 waits with the 1405 to Exeter St Davids. The banner on the footbridge reads 'Devon County Council and Dartmoor Railway celebrating 10 years of success'. 17 June 2007.

A further picture from the Dartmoor Archive, this one very much in to the final days of the LSWR. The station staff pose for a picture on the down, i.e. Plymouth bound platform. At the end of the timber-framed building with its fine slate roof, Spiers and Pond who had the contract with the LSWR to operate its dining cars and most of their station refreshment rooms invite one's custom. Here we also see the original signal box. Circa 1920.

A similar scene on the former down platform today, the awning added in early 1930s. The cramped signal box was replaced by one on the up platform on the west side of the footbridge in 1936 to simplify the workings of the station. D4167 and its train wait with the 1415 to Meldon Viaduct. 5 August 2018.

The Fatherford Tramway

Opposite the entrance to Okehampton Station is a signpost bearing the legend 'Footpath to Fatherford Viaduct' directing one through a green gate and down a lengthy and steep flight of steps to the gravel footpath shown in the photo above. This was the start of Fatherford Tramway which ran for just under one mile. Little is known of it in its working life and no photographs have come to light. A narrow gauge line (precise gauge unknown) worked by horses ran from Okehampton Station goods yard by a short steep spur, which is almost certainly the muddy bank behind the gate we see to the right, after reversal to serve the quarries near to Fatherford Viaduct. It was built c.1870 by either the Devon & Cornwall Railway or its contractor and may well have provided stone for the railway. It is known in the early 1900s two quarries in the vicinity of the viaduct were served by the line. The 1912 edition of Crossing's *Guide to Dartmoor* mentions part of the walk from Okehampton Station to Fatherford Viaduct is partly on an old tramway. It was used in the First War to transport pit props cut in the valley down to the station, and after an unknown closure date lifted in the 1930s. Its course lay derelict until fairly recent times when it was restored as a footpath, running from beneath the station in the valley through Tramlines Wood, so named by the Woodland Trust. Leaving the shade of the trees the path has a more open feel, before making a right hand turn. The tramway is known to have passed under the viaduct which formerly marked the northern boundary of the National Park until it was altered to accommodate the Okehampton bypass, so it makes it as a Dartmoor Railway by a matter of yards. The tramway's legacy is this short pleasant footpath. 31 July 2018.

The arrival of the railway on northern Dartmoor did not go unnoticed by the military. The means to transport large numbers of men, horses, equipment, guns and munitions was now a reality and from 1873 Dartmoor began to be used by the army for large-scale manoeuvres. In 1875 a committee was set up to examine the training of field artillery units under service conditions. On 23 June 1875 two members of the committee visited Dartmoor to seek a suitable site for a practice camp and the land high above Okehampton ticked all the boxes. The first annual exercise began in 1876 when the Royal Artillery pitched a camp at Halstock Down for a three-week period, later increased to six weeks. In 1886 the Drill Ground Act was passed which gave the War Department powers to acquire land for artillery and rifle ranges. In 1890 the Public and General Act extended these powers. Meanwhile the War Department had been acquiring the necessary leases and the construction of a permanent camp above Okehampton began in July 1892, with the first phase completed 14 June 1894. To facilitate this and provide space for loading and unloading away from the station, the up siding was extended westward to form a set of three sidings; two of them serving an island platform with run-round facilities incorporated. These became known as Okehampton Military Sidings. Batteries arrived by rail with their own horses. At the turn of the century a battery comprised five officers, 166 men with six guns and at least 89 horses required for the two week stay. These two historic photographs from the Dartmoor Trust Archive shows a scene of great activity as a troop train is unloaded; usually these were split in to two for unloading as in the photo above we see the passenger coaches for the men held in the shorter of the island platforms to the left.

A motley collection of vehicles is on show in the photograph above. Note in the longer of the two platforms to the right, immediately behind the two passenger coaches (probably reserved for officers), two short-wheelbase LSWR horse boxes used to transport the officer's horses, the small chimneys on each to allow the officers servants accompanying their horses some degree of comfort. Behind there is a rake of cattle trucks used to transport the light and heavy horses. Study-

ing the pictures, the cap badges suggest this is the Royal Artillery, and looking at the covered loads these are more than likely field guns and their limbers. We can date the pictures to no earlier than 1910 as clearly visible is the brand new hut for A. C. Culley (of Cardiff) who were granted in that year (at a rent of £2 per annum) a license to serve refreshments and rations to the troops.

The Military Sidings found a new use for four years when they were adapted as the terminal for the Surbiton-Okehampton Car Carrier, ideal as the train could be split and stabled clear of the main line, complete with a ready-made platform for driving cars in and out of the GUV vehicles. Military traffic at Okehampton had been in decline for sometime as the needs of the army changed, although it continued in to the mid 1970s. All such activity is a thing of the past as (below) 142 015+142 016 pass by on the PRC run Dartmoor Boundaryman Rail Tour, the sidings demolished, the weeds in control and only the former down main line survives to serve Meldon Quarry. The view is from Tor Bridge, the road a long climb up to the High Moor and the army camp. 31 May 1987.

Today there is little evidence that the Military Sidings ever existed, the first of the two Portacabins is the home of Okehampton Detachment of the Army Cadet Force, the second the Air Training Corps 2443 Okehampton Squadron, so there is still an armed service presence here. On what is now just a single-line country railway the latest incarnation of the Dartmoor Railway Meldon shuttle, D4167 leading with behind RDB975046+S13436+731411, drift past with the 1555 Meldon Viaduct-Okehampton. 5 August 2018.

We turn and look the other way from Tor Road Bridge with 68006 working hard pushing 80225 +61743 up the hill with the 1320 Okehampton-Meldon. The single line occupies the former down main line, the up one at this point in time undergoing transformation into the foot and cycle path which we shall see in its completed state when we return here at a lower level for the second appearance of steam on the Meldon shuttle. 3 June 2001.

Okehampton Military Railways: The Okehampton Target Railway – East Mill Tor to Skit Bottom

We now pay a visit to the High Moor directly above Okehampton to see how the military made its mark with its own little railways. In 1895 an additional 10,000 acres of the High Moor was leased from the Duchy of Cornwall. This was at the time of the Boer Wars, and to counter the tactics used by the Boers trenches were dug to determine methods of attacking defensive positions. On the Okehampton range, four targets railways have existed at various times. The first, the longest at just over a half a mile in length, and the only one to incorporate an incline, was the Okehampton Target Railway, thought to be constructed in 1895 running from the eastern side of East Mill Tor to Skit Bottom, 450 feet south of East Okement Farm. Observation Post 6 (OP6) and the target railway are first shown on a military OS Map of Okehampton in 1898. The moving target operated as a series of trolleys (thought to be ten in number) that would run from the top of the track by OP6 the length of the tramway by means of gravity. Targets positioned on the top of the moving trolleys would then be fired on by artillery guns, thought to have been positioned along Oke Tor Ridge 2400 feet to the east. The trolleys would then be pulled back up the hill by horses and the operation would start again. The gauge of the line was one foot eighteen inches; it predated the military loop road built 1906-07 which still exists. The view below is looking across what would have been the level crossing with the road, with East Mill Tor behind the photographer. The course of the line on the other side of the road is clearly defined curving away to the left towards Skit Bottom. Storm clouds gather over Higher Tor. In the foreground and to the right of the gorse bush a small section of track which was of flat bottom rail is clearly visible, a surprising and gratifying discovery. 31 July 2018.

A photograph dated c.1916 from the Dartmoor Trust Archive shows members of the Royal Field Artillery at the firing ranges above Okehampton where the target railway was in use. The railway was later used for anti-tank training, its closure date unknown, with the rails removed in 1982.

Crossing the military loop road the photograph below shows the opposite view from that on the previous page, looking west with East Mill Tor providing the back drop. The course of the former railway is to the immediate right of the photographer and easily discernable on the other side of the road in its ditch. The precise height here is 1350 feet above sea level; the grid reference is 603904. The course of the former railway is easily followed a short distance up the hill to the still surviving Observation Post No 6. These small railways built above Okehampton and also those we shall encounter at Willsworthy, were built under the auspices of the War Department, transferring to the Ministry of Defence from 1 April 1964. A suitable day for the civil servants in Whitehall to take control? 31 July 2018.

The Rowtor Target Railway, high above Okehampton, is a unique survivor. Until the Second War, the only target railway on the Okehampton Range had been the former East Mill Tor to Skit Bottom line. Near to the start of the Second World War, a 2' 6" gauge target railway was built to the east of West Mill Tor. At some time around 1942 this line was closed and demolished, although its former course can still be traced and is best described as a furrow running in a north easterly direction. It was replaced by a new line constructed to the south east of the original, known as the Rowtor Target Railway at Grid Reference SX593910. Built to a gauge of 2 '6" the line is 500 yards in length. Its layout is simple, starting on a balloon loop which has a spur to its shed; the line enters a straight and shallow cutting across the Dartmoor heath, before taking the curve which leads to a further balloon loop. The layout of the railway is best described as a dumbbell-shaped design with continuous loops at either end, allowing the unmanned trolley with its wooden target in the shape of a military tank to be run continuously. It is known the railway survived at least in to the early 1970s, and some restoration work was carried out around 2002. Of all the railways built upon the High Moor, it is the lone survivor and remains more or less intact. At 1510 feet above sea level it is one of the highest narrow gauge railways in England.

Sturdily built of local materials the double track locomotive shed of the Rowtor Target Railway was served by a spur off its western balloon loop. It still serves its original purpose of housing rolling stock with Wickham Trolley number 767138 *Captain* inside. Its former companion Wickham Trolley unnamed 767139 is preserved on the Leighton Buzzard narrow gauge railway. Sadly *Captain* rarely sees daylight as the shed is permanently locked, and photographs of it are hard to come by. 5 September 2018.

Basic infrastructure at its best; a point lever and lightweight track heading east through the shallow ditch, cut through the heath to give protection against falling shot on this stretch of the line. Geography suggests firing would have come from the right hand side from this viewpoint. 5 September 2018.

The end east of the shallow ditch. The track bends on a gentle curve at the start of the eastern balloon loop, behind rises the 1736 feet high West Mill Tor. The fourth of the Okehampton military target railways was situated at Blackdown. This is out of camera range to the top left of the view, the only remnants are a furrow running under the Tor in a north-easterly direction. 5 September 2018.

A classic Dartmoor scene, the rusting rails of the eastern balloon loop with East Mill Tor as a backdrop. 5 September 2018.

The arc of the eastern balloon loop; the background is a familiar setting as the view is looking towards Higher Tor, behind this to the left is Belstone Tor. To the right is the southern ridge of Oke Tor and the trees between the railway and the Tors are adjacent to East Okement Farm. The East Mill Tor to Skit Bottom line lay in between down in the valley. 5 September 2018.

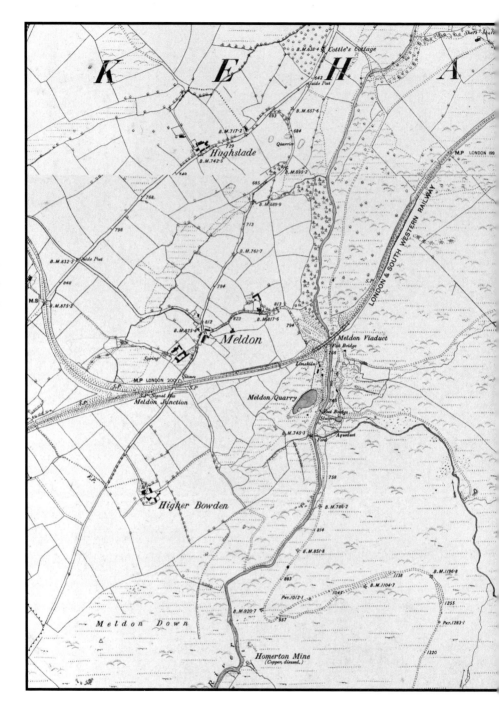

Above: Back to the SR main line and the climb away from the Military Sidings to Meldon to see only the second steam engine to work the Meldon Shuttle in the Dartmoor Railway era. 30075 makes a fine sight propelling 59520 and 731411 up the hill. 30075 is one of the Yugoslavian built tanks, a design imported in to Europe during the Second World War of which 14 subsequently came to the Southern Railway. Known as USA tanks, on nationalisation they were numbered 30061-74.They were ideally suited to dock shunting especially at Southampton, although as we shall see one made it to literally to just up the road from here. Acquired by Project 52 as JZ 62-669 from Store Steel in Slovenia, the engine took the next available number in the series. Compare with the shot of 68006 taken from the road bridge here, the cycle path now occupies the former up line and a sturdy fence now separates the Lycra from the railway. 24 August 2010.

Opposite: Detail from the 1885 Ordnance Survey map of the LSWR route from Okehampton to Meldon Junction where the line branched off to Holsworthy. At this date Meldon Quarry was less extensive than it later became. The Dartmoor Trust Archive.

Northern Dartmoor proved not only to be useful to the military, its minerals proved to be ideal for use by the railway. Briefly, the stone at Meldon is found in a metamorphic zone, the majority of the metamorphic rocks occurring here are known as hornfels When blended together correctly have the ideal properties for high quality railway ballast. This became apparent as the LSWR excavated the cuttings here in the construction of the line to Lydford when the hornfels were exposed.

A small quarry opened here with the line in 1874 to supply local railway requirements, it was considerably expanded in 1897, Meldon stone was found to be of the best quality of all the sources available to the LSWR. It was further extended in 1902 eventually covering 200 acres. By 1907, 107,000 tons of stone per annum was extracted from Meldon. Production continued apace through the SR and BR eras, at the time of nationalisation 1000 tons of stone a day was taken from the quarry.

After the 1994 takeover by ECC Quarries (CAMAS Aggregates later the same year) the stone traffic flourished. For example in 1997 there were up to five ballast trains a day leaving the quarry. But market forces took their toll and the quarry closed in 2008, the infrastructure demolished in 2011. The quarry had its own shunting engine, and this was the last place west of Exeter where working steam could be seen. Taken from a passing train we see USA 0-6-0 Tank DS 234 the former 30062 (30075 would not have been out of place at Meldon) to the right of its concrete shed. Behind on the hill just look at that infrastructure, a classic busy quarry scene. 14 June 1965.

The updated view is directly opposite the Meldon Viaduct station of today, the commanding link between the two images is the former concrete locomotive shed, and to the right some of the point and track work survives. Where have that hill and its busy workings gone? 5 August 2018.

Built partially on the site of the former Quarry Halt, the only station open for timetabled passenger trains within the National Park is Meldon Viaduct, opened as Meldon Quarry on 6 July 2002, adopting the present name in July 2015. Class 205 unit 1132 waits in a sylvan setting more akin to leafy Surrey with the 1630 to Okehampton. 7 June 2009.

The *piece de resistance* of the SR route is Meldon Viaduct, taking the line on a 1 in 77 gradient on a right hand curve of 30 chains radius with a maximum height of 151 feet over the valley of the West Okement River. Originally a single line structure, when the route was doubled in 1879, in simple terms a second identical viaduct was built on the south flank with entwined piers. What to the eye is a double-track line structure of wrought iron lattice piers to support the cast iron trusses is in fact two separate single-line structures side by side.

This view in 1890 from Francis Frith allows us to study the valley's industrial use on both sides of the river. Research of this and the associated tramways has proved difficult, only approximate dates can be quoted and OS Maps have proved to be inconclusive. From left to right we start with the lime kiln. A limestone quarry in the valley adjacent to the west bank of the river was established around 1885, its site now a pond. A short narrow gauge tramway thought to be 2 feet gauge connected the two. To the right of the lime kiln is the access road, beneath lay the West Okement River above which is the leat to the glassworks. On the eastern bank of the river, also in the 1880s, a valuable source of aplite with ideal qualities for glass making was found in the area. A further aplite quarry, separate to the railway stone quarry and at a lower level, was leased in 1885 by a Charles Green. This quarry which today remains visible with some of its buildings is between the stone quarry and Meldon Dam. Next to the leat is the horse-worked tramway established from this quarry (again a gauge of 2 or 3 feet is disputed) its rails prefabricated in 12 feet lengths to carry the granulite in tip-trucks, and these are visible in the photograph at the tramway's terminus.

To the far right is the incline ascending to a point now opposite the present-day Meldon Viaduct station, this would make sense as the 1899 OS Map shows a narrow gauge line of the Meldon Valley Company leaving a loading bank at the west end of the railway quarry and descending into the valley where it appears to split in to two tracks.

The aplite was exported by rail to destinations such as the Potteries. In 1920 came a new industry to Dartmoor, glass production. A glass-bottle works was set up in the valley out of camera range to the right of the photo. There were high hopes of this becoming a major industry for the area and over 100 people were employed. Impurities in the locally quarried minerals hampered the production of clear glass and production appears to have ceased in February 1921. It is known the Southern Railway in July 1923 were aware of the Meldon Valley Company being in receivership; this would appear to be the conclusion of industrial activity in the valley at Meldon. 1890, © Francis Frith Collection.

It is a fortunate coincidence that 78 years after Francis Frith took his picture in the Meldon Valley that I (unaware at the time of the existence of the original) stood more or less in the same place to record a train passing over the viaduct in the final weeks of the passenger service. There was still evidence of man making his mark on the scene as, overhead, a two-car DMU heads west with the 1330 Exeter St Davids–Plymouth. Looking again from left to right, the remains of the former lime kiln can be spotted, the West Okement River still flows but there is little evidence of the leat or the tramway and the works associated with materials for glass. One can just about make out the site of the tramway on the far right up to the main line. A corresponding view today would show the viaduct crossing what now is best described as a tree plantation; growth in the valley has now to-tally obliterated any signs of industry and those little railways. 24 April 1968.

Meldon Viaduct is one of the only two surviving railway bridges in the country to use wrought iron lattice piers to support the cast iron trusses, the other being Bennerley Viaduct, on the former Northern Railway Derby extension, over the Erewash Valley marking the country boundaries between Awsworth in Nottinghamshire and Ilkeston in Derbyshire. This view, looking west from the north side, clearly shows the entwined piers of the twin viaducts as 34020 *Seaton* crosses with the 1652 Plymouth–Eastleigh.

Following the line's closure, a temporary road was laid over the viaduct in 1970 for the use of lorries taking aggregate for the construction of the nearby Meldon Dam. Despite the condition of the viaduct being one of the reasons cited for closing the line, in 1978 the former up line was reopened as an additional head shunt space for the quarry, this lasting until 1990. Six years later it was refurbished, the new owners CAMAS and the BR Property Board sharing the cost. The steel structure was completely sand blasted and painted, new railings and a timber deck fitted and repairs to the masonry undertaken. In 1997 the structure was sold to Devon County Council for a £1, in 1998 The Meldon Viaduct Company was formed to take responsibility for the structure which in the following year became part of the Granite Way when the cycleway over it was opened. Will we ever see another train pass over this graceful structure? 7 September 1963.

The railway on the northern edge of Dartmoor, with the North Cornwall line curving away to the left, 34096 *Trevone* approaches Meldon Junction with the 1652 Plymouth–Eastleigh. Behind the train stands Yes Tor, at 2031 feet above sea level; the second highest point on Dartmoor. To its left is West Mill Tor at 1774 feet. The train has not long emerged from Darkey's Cutting at Sourton where the summit of the line at 950 feet is reached. This is often misquoted by many as the highest point on the former Southern Railway system, This was so for the standard gauge but higher still at 973 feet is Woody Bay in Exmoor on the restored section of the narrow gauge 1 foot 11½" inch Lynton and Barnstaple Railway.

Trevone was built as a Bulleid Pacific in the original form at Brighton Works emerging in November 1949. The engine was rebuilt at Eastleigh Works emerging in April 1961 and sent to work off Exmouth Junction (Exeter) shed. Such was the carnage at the time to the steam fleet; this was the last working for *Trevone*. Detached from the 1652 at Exeter Central on reaching Exmouth Junction the fire was dropped and the engine withdrawn soon after being surplus to requirements. A rebuilt engine just 3 years old with decades of work left in it consigned to the scrapheap at the stroke of the accountant's pen. 29 August 1964.

The Rattlebrook Peat Railway

The SR main line descends mostly past Sourton at 1 in 82 to Bridestowe Station, where we encounter another of those mineral lines built to tap the resources of the higher parts of Dartmoor. The Rattlebrook Peat Railway was built to serve a not entirely successful commercial operation of extracting a great natural resource of which much is found on the High Moor.

History: In 1878 extensive peat works were opened between Great Links Tor and Kitty Tor on the bleak slopes of the north-western Moor. The Rattlebrook Peat Railway was built for the Duchy of Cornwall for use by the Dartmoor Compressed Peat Company, and was actually surveyed by the LSWR. Alterations to the layout at Bridestowe station to accommodate the new line were advised to the Board of Trade by the LSWR on 26 June 1880, the likely opening date of the route. It was not long belong financial problems beset the company and the railway had a fairly short continuous career although operations continued spasmodically into the 20th century. The peat works ceased production in the late 1920s and the rails were lifted in 1931–32. After the demolition lorries were occasionally used to bring down peat from the moor, the last peat being loaded at Bridestowe Station in about 1955 for onward transit to Guernsey.

Route: As the crow flies it is about 2½ miles from Bridestowe station to the Peat Works at Rattlebrook. Beginning from sidings at the north end of Bridestowe station the standard gauge line followed a zigzag course of seven miles, climbing 800 feet in the process. The climb started immediately upon leaving the LSWR and about 200 yards north of the junction the line crossed the A386 road on the level by Cranford Bridge, curving away to the right up to Nodden Gate where a long curve took the line in effect to run in the other direction through Great Nodden, utilising the Lyd Valley for the climb to a remote reversal point best described as being above Coombe Down. This was also the only passing point on the route, which rather limited line capacity and goes some way to explaining how at best a maximum of six wagons a day were handed over to the LSWR at Bridestowe.

From the zigzag reversal the line climbed steadily past Great Links Tor and Kitty Tor reaching its summit. A short descent from here brought the line to its terminus at Rattlebrook where a varied collection of buildings and kilns processed the peat for drying. This was brought down to a central point from the cuttings by a system of narrow gauge tramways. At its peak 100 men found employment here, a bleak place to work indeed. The legacy of the Rattlebrook Peat Railway is a very fine footpath ideal for exploring this remote part of Dartmoor.

The line was horse-worked except for its final couple or so years when it was worked by a lorry, this being kept in a garage by the gate at Bridestowe Station. Its road wheels were removed and replaced by flanged rail wheels in what must have been one of the more unusual jobs for a garage in Okehampton. The lorry was used to demolish the line in 1932. Photographs of the Rattlebrook Peat Railway in operation are very few in number.

The 1727 Exeter St Davids–Plymouth runs into Bridestowe passing the exchange sidings with the Rattlebrook Peat Railway, whose course climbing away from the station is very discernable from behind the train. 23 April 1968.

I have only once walked the full length of the line and that was on a dull Sunday in June 1972. This is the view looking north up to Great Nodden; the River Lyd is on the right.

Climbing higher to Great Nodden, this is the view looking the other way down the River Lyd which is to the left. Gibbet Hill can be seen on the horizon on the left, with Brentor in the centre right. The course of the Peat Railway is clearly evident, the line following the contours. June 1972.

The reversing point situated roughly half away along the line. With Great Nodden to the right and Arms Tor in the centre, the gradual S bend of the line climbing up from Bridestowe makes it way over the moorland to reach the line coming down the hill from Rattlebrook, this coming in to the left of the picture, to the far right the start of what would have been the passing loop. June 1972.

This is the view from the summit of the line looking down the incline to the terminus at Rattlebrook. The ruins of the clay works are in the middle distance; behind them is Amicombe Hill with Kitty Tor on the horizon. June 1972.

A couple of miles on from Bridestowe station, the 1315 Plymouth–Exeter St Davids approaches School Road over bridge, this carrying the road from the adjacent A386 to Lydford village barely half a mile distant to the right. Our next port of call is a diversion to the hills in the distance on the extreme left to Willsworthy to examine the Target Railways. 23 April 1968.

It is not often one can take a picture of a railway and get its whole length in the frame, but such is the case with the 2'3" gauge Willsworthy Target Railway situated in the shadow of White Hill at 1168 feet above sea level. Of the nine known military target railways to have been constructed on Dartmoor, this is the only one which remains in use. The military involvement at Willsworthy can be said to have started in the early years of the last century. The 1912 edition of Crossing's *Guide to Dartmoor* comments 'It is a matter of regret that such a charming part of Dartmoor should be robbed of its quietude and solitariness, but much of it has lately been acquired by the War Office for rifle practice'. The proximity of Lydford station barely two miles distant served by both the GWR and the LSWR was no doubt a factor in the establishment the camp. The ranges at Willsworthy were modernised and slightly reoriented in 1983–84 when the present day target railway was installed. 31 July 2018.

Army encampment at Willsworthy c.1915.
The Dartmoor Trust Archive

Prior to the present day installation, there were four other target railways that have existed on or about the range, their history lost in the mists of time. The view below is looking east from the troop shelter. To the top right it is more or less in front of the white target wall that a target tramway is shown on the 1950s Ordnance Survey map running down to the right of the picture and terminating by a mine leat. No trace whatsoever of this has been found. In the centre of the picture a well defined track can be seen and this is the site of a target tramway which commenced just short of the present day 200 yard marker for the targets that pop up in front of the white wall at Grid Reference 52830 83333, at 1130 feet above sea level. This line was 363 yards in length. A ditch behind the troop shelter marks its terminus. Neither of these appear in the OS Maps of the 1900s, but both appear on the 1950s maps which would suggest these may well have been in use around both before, certainly in and likely immediately after the Second World War. 7 September 2018.

The third and the oldest of the disused military railways of Willsworthy is remote from the present-day operation and the two already mentioned disused ones. Taking one's bearings from the target white wall mentioned in the top picture, behind this is the current building used by the military. Opposite this turn left off the tarmac road on to a track which descends down in to the valley, it is about half a mile walk. At the bottom of the hill cross the ford and continue up the hill a very short distance through a field to a very prominent stile.

The view from the stile, in the foreground is the eastern end of what I would call the Redford Farm Target Railway Number 1, a name I have created just to distinguish this one from the others past and present. Redford Farm was occupied until purchased by the military in 1904 who established Willsworthy training camp in 1908. The nearby farm house is known to have been derelict by 1910 when a target railway alongside a corn ditch to the east of the house was established. The hole in the foreground is the walled pit which housed the winding gear for the moving target, and the line was controlled from here.

Descending into the pit was a revelation. It was the northern observation post constructed in a sturdy bunker with relics visible, the two sets of wire, each emanating from connection boxes with their severed exit cables hanging loose. One is certainly for electricity; the second could be a telephone connection. The style of equipment suggest circa World War Two vintage, so this is possibly a clue as to when the tramway ceased operation. The latter appears on the 1950s OS maps. Jeremy Clark, both 7 September 2018.

The view looking west towards Nattor Down showing the whole length of the line. It starts at Grid Reference 5377983256 at 1109 feet above sea level. The gauge is two feet and total length 164 yards. The line terminates at Grid Reference 53757 83099 at 1087 feet above sea level, in its short course it drops 22 feet. The line runs beside the fields of the former farm to the left where sheep still graze.
7 September 2018.

Further relics of the line can be found at its southern end opposite what would have been the underground observation post. These are levers and rodding which would have displayed the indication whether to fire or not, controlled from rods at each observation post at both ends of the line. 7 September 2018.

Opposite: Looking at a detailed 1950's map of the area, a second target railway was shown just to the north of the one we had previously visited at Redford Farm. In previous publications, various authors have suggested three target railways pre-dated the present installation, only the one to the north-east of the range having any surviving track. Curiosity was aroused and we ventured again to Redford and after some considerable effort found the second target railway, its course clearly evident. At the bottom end, where some track is still to be seen, was another pit that proved to be the observation post complete with redundant connecting boxes and cabling still visible. To take our bearings from Redford Farm Target Railway Number 1, this is just out of camera range to the far right of the picture opposite and about 200 yards separates the two lines. The wall and ditch to the left of it mark the course of the second railway. They run parallel to each other and are of equal length of 200 yards, were of the same gauge of 2 feet and operated with the same principal of controlled rods to give the indication of whether to fire or not. It is likely both were constructed around the same time, but if they became disused at the same time is unknown. Both are now overgrown and the remaining track appears in places out of the grass and the gorse. What we shall now christen Redford Farm Target Railway Number 2 has been disused for a long time, but does its appearance on the early 1950s map provide a clue? 15 September 2018 Jeremy Clark.

The south end of the railway comes to an abrupt end in the grass, the pit for the former observation post is more or less in front of the last rocks forming the boundary of the route. These surviving rails are evidence of the line's existence. 15 September 2018 Jeremy Clark.

At Lydford we meet the GWR Launceston Branch whose history I will discuss later. Above, 5564 arrives with the 1040 from Plymouth, the SR station to the right, the GWR one the summit of its line at 650 feet to the left. 22 December 1962, the late Peter Gray, now Great Western Trust Collection.

Lydford was not a joint station, nor from 1890–1943 a junction either. After the LSW gained its own route to Plymouth, the connection between the two systems was removed in 1895. Originally named Lidford the present name was adopted by both companies in July 1897. The two stations existed side by side as separate entities. Due to the manpower demands of the First World War, as from 1 March 1914 the LSWR took over the staffing and supervision of the GWR station. On 8 January 1917, the LSWR signal box, which was at the Okehampton end of the station, and the GWR signal box which was at the Plymouth end, were both closed and replaced by a new structure, built on the central platform each half over the agreed boundary between the companies, with back-to-back frames. It was worked by the LSWR later SR signalman, with SR supervision of the station remaining throughout the SR and BR eras. The Second World War saw the station at its busiest enhanced by the greater use of Willsworthy by the military. In 1943 substantial alterations took place when the direct connection between the systems was brought in to use as from 21 June 1943. The new sidings installed on the SR side were laid partially on the SR approach road; passenger access to their side of the station was thence by the GWR approach and a foot crossing over the GWR line. The sidings were used mainly for the berthing of ammunitions, the theory being that if hit by enemy action, the damage would be less severe on remote Dartmoor than in a city such as Plymouth. Post war as military use of the Moor returned to normal, the sidings were left in use often accommodating surplus rolling stock. The war time connection also remained, and saw regular use particularly on Sundays when the Lifton milk train ran by way of the SR route from Plymouth to reverse on to the GWR branch.

The corresponding view looking towards Launceston and Okehampton shows there is little to remind one of the twin stations. Growth hinders the view of Great Links Tor. Could one really go four ways from here by train where only a boggy field is now all there is to be seen? 25 March 2017.

The two railways ran parallel from Lydford down the valley of the River Burn until it meets the Tavy. The GWR felt Brentor only merited goods siding installed in 1866. When the PDSWJR built their route from Lydford to Devonport for the LSWR, they chose to serve Brentor ,the station opening with the line .The GWR simply passed by the back of the station. The station survives as a private residence with plenty of nostalgic reminders of its past. The top view is looking towards Tavistock, the lower towards Lydford, both date from the Edwardian era c.1912.

About a mile or so further on was Mary Tavy, served only by the GWR Launceston Branch, the SR main line passing behind it in a cutting, the LSWR road bridge parapet is visible in the lower photo immediately to the right of the roof of the station house. It opened with the Launceston extension. To provide extra capacity

for the LSWR invasion, a signal box, crossing loop and an additional platform were installed in 1876, these taken out of use in 1895. The and Blackdown part of the name was added in 1907, the station was equidistant from each village but this renaming was more to attract walkers and hikers to the nearby Moor. The small goods siding and yard at the Lydford end of the station was in closed in December 1948, in its latter days it was only used by a local farmer.

Immediately behind in the field above the wagons in the yard the SR line cutting can be made out running above the signal box to the roof of the station building. The station buildings and former signal box would survive until the station closed, while the station cottage, seen above, remains in use as a private residence. c.1914, The Dartmoor Trust Archive

From where the two railways from Lydford enter the Tavy Valley near Peter Tavy, they exit Dartmoor and make their separate ways to Tavistock, a border town between Dartmoor and the Tavy and Tamar Valleys and a gateway to each. High above the town was the SR station, Tavistock North seen in the photograph above (taken 1 May 1968) is looking towards Okehampton with the 1624 to Bere Alston awaiting the 100+ school children and the shoppers to join in the last week of operation, from the following Monday they would all have to travel in four buses. The photo below from The Dartmoor Trust Archive shows a deserted station also from 1968. Note the Scottish-designed footbridge now in store on the Plym Valley Railway awaiting restoration and the fine co-acting arm signal behind.

Seen from Glanville Road, the 1624 Tavistock North-Bere Alston crosses the eight arch Kilworthy Viaduct, 420 feet in length with a maximum height of 70 feet; Cox Tor provides an impressive backdrop as we leave the SR main line. 1 May 1968.

The line from Meldon to Bere Alston was demolished over the autumn/winter 1969-70, in the early 1990s a footpath was created over the viaduct and through the cutting which runs behind where the photographer was standing. This still exists as a very pleasant walk. Notice how houses have been built on the track bed between the viaduct and the station. This is a 1995 update; the view today impossible due to growth. 18 May 1995.

The BR timetables for each line contained next to the relevant station a note usually the letter 'A' which read 1 mile to Tavistock South station, and vice versa. So let us take the SR advice and walk down Kilworthy Hill, through the town square and over Abbey Bridge, seen here in its setting above the weir on the River Tavy. The green box notes the point where water is extracted from the River Tavy to supply the Tavistock Canal. 5 March 1967.

Over Abbey Bridge and a short walk up Whitchurch Road we return to the GWR branch at Tavistock South to continue our journey to Plymouth. This was the principal intermediate station on the line and also its busiest. This view is looking towards Plymouth, 5569 takes water working the 1040 Plymouth–Launceston. To the right is the large goods shed. 22 December 1962, the late Peter Gray, now Great Western Trust Collection.

On 22 June 1859 the South Devon & Tavistock Railway Company opened their broad gauge line from a junction on the SDR main line near Marsh Mills to Tavistock, trains running to and from the SDR Millbay Terminus. Intermediate stations were provided at Bickleigh and Horrabridge, Marsh Mills was added in 1861. Another subsidiary of the SDR completed the extension to Launceston opening on 1 June 1865, with intermediate stations provided at Mary Tavy, Lidford, Coryton and Lifton. Public traffic actually commenced on the Launceston extension a month later on 1 July 1865, the delay being due to the Board of Trade Inspector requiring some minor problems to be corrected. On this same day the South Devon & Tavistock was taken over by the South Devon Railway. The Launceston Company was absorbed by the SDR on 24 June 1869 with amalgamation occurring on 31 December 1873. The SDR was amalgamated with the GWR as from 1 February 1876. (The line's part in the story of the battle for railway supremacy in the South west as the LSWR spread its tentacles further west has already been already been told). After the LSWR invasion the line returned to its role as just another GWR branch line. A major event in those 14 years occurred on 11 August 1883 with the opening of the Princetown Branch, more of which later. The line was converted to standard gauge over the weekend of 20–22 May 1892.

The turn of the century brought the awakening of the GWR to local travel. with many halts springing up throughout the system – the Tavistock Branch being no exception. Whitchurch gained one in 1906, yet Clearbrook, where the railway passed directly by the village, had to wait until 1928! The Branch ran through some lovely wooded valleys and to tap their potential for walkers, hikers and day trippers further halts were provided at Plym Bridge in 1906 and Shaugh Bridge in 1907. These stations and halts between Plym Bridge and Yelverton would become a part of everyday life for the people of Plymouth. Between the two Wars, peaking in the 1930s, on Wednesday afternoons, summer evenings, Sundays and Bank Holidays the GWR ran 'Woolworth's Specials' (the fare to any station between Plym Bridge and Yelverton was 6d), and the passengers came literally in their thousands.

Upon nationalisation at the start of 1948 the line passed to the Western Region of British Railways. However, the branch was vulnerable to the growing motor age. The Princetown Branch closed completely as from 5 March 1956 and ,despite howls of protest, the branch passenger service was withdrawn as from 31 December 1962, the day before Dr Beeching took office as Chairman of the British Railways Board. Marsh Mills–Tavistock South and Lifton–Launceston closed completely. Lydford–Tavistock South and Lydford–Lifton were retained for freight, and transferred to the Southern Region. Thus Waterloo had at long last taken back a part of its former route to Plymouth. But the victory was short lived as all SR lines west of Wilton South (the first station to the west of Salisbury) were transferred to the Western Region from 1 January 1963. Marsh Mills–Tavistock South was demolished in the spring of 1964. To allow for withdrawal of the North

Cornwall line freight service, Lifton-Launceston was reopened as from 7 September 1964. Tavistock South–Lydford closed completely as from 25 September 1964. Lydford–Launceston was closed completely as from 28 February 1966.

The Plym Valley Railway Association was formed on 20 February 1980. After what was a long and painful birth, the superhuman efforts of its volunteers bore fruit. At Marsh Mills a new station was built about 200 yards north of the original and levels altered, a new junction was created at Marsh Mills North to serve the sidings and provide a base for the venture. Three masonry bridges were restored, a level crossing constructed to take the cycle path over the railway at a new Lee Moor Crossing, a new station at Plym Bridge constructed as well as some considerable civil engineering undertaken. The restored line opened in stages as work progressed and the required money raised. Marsh Mills to World's End, a point about 200 yards north of Marsh Mills North Junction, reopening 14 October 2001, World's End to Lee Moor Crossing (but not across it) 24 May 2008, Lee Moor Crossing to Plym Bridge (where a new station was built on the site of the original) was reopened on 30 December 2012, fifty years and a day after its original closure. Thus in the shadow of Dartmoor one can now once again enjoy hearing the sound of hissing steam and piston crank in the woods between Marsh Mills and Plym Bridge, following in the footsteps of the 'Woolworths Specials'. An in-depth study of the line then and now can be found in the author's book *Back Tracking Around the Plymouth–Tavistock South–Launceston Branch*.

This remarkable contribution is from The Dartmoor Trust Archive shows the GWR station at Tavistock after the devastating fire of 1887; this is one of the few showing the line in the era of the mixed gauge between Lydford and Tavistock Junction. The dual-gauge rails are clearly visible. After the fire of 1887 the station was rebuilt to the same stone and wood construction. Many who since cast their eyes over the fine wooden overall roof were probably unaware they were not looking at the Brunel inspired original but an 1888 replica.

We resume our journey to Plymouth by way of the Launceston branch which between here and Plym Bridge hugged the edge of the Western moor for much of its course. Tavistock South was very convenient for the town centre and it was also a fairly large installation. The view looking towards Launceston, the goods shed to the left. It was at Tavistock South in a fearful blizzard on the last night of the branch (29/30 December 1962) that 5568 arrived at 0020, five hours late with the 1820 Plymouth-Launceston after a heroic battle with the elements where the train was abandoned. The snow had claimed the final victory over the Branch as this should have been the penultimate train to run the whole route. 6430 awaits departure with the 1400 empty stock to Plymouth Millbay. 23 June 1962, the late Peter Gray, now Great Western Trust Collection.

The station was demolished in 1968 has been completely eradicated. This updated view looks towards the fire station and the Doctor's surgery. June 2017.

Our journey south re-enters the National Park at Whitchurch, its station Whitchurch Down Platform, opened on 1 September 1906, indicating its purpose was not only to serve the village, but also to attract walkers and hikers to the local beauty spot on the moor about a mile up the hill to the east. This was indeed successful bringing much business to the GWR and no doubt the local pub. The Dartmoor Trust Archive.

Below 6438 is captured leaving with an auto train for Tavistock, note the square corrugated waiting shelter situated roughly in the middle of the rather lengthy station. The platform still survives but is completely engulfed by a combination of extended gardens from the houses in Whitchurch Road and substantial natural growth. 23 June 1962, the late R.C. Riley, the Transport Trust.

The route between Whitchurch and Horrabridge negotiating the Walkham Valley required two viaducts and a tunnel. Below: 48 chains before crossing its more famous neighbour, Walkham Viaduct, a train from Plymouth would traverse the 216 yard Magpie Viaduct. Built of Blue Staffordshire brick, opening in 1902, it replaced the previous timber viaduct here with a maximum height of 62 feet. An unidentified 45XX tank is seen heading for Launceston probably on the 1212 from Plymouth with an unusual consist of six coaches. Today it is still possible to traverse the structure and enjoy the views looking towards the moor as it forms part of the Drakes Cycle path. c.1956, Ian H. Lane.

Horrabridge looking towards Yelverton in the Edwardian era, at the southern end of the station is the level crossing over the road from Buckland Monachorum; its gates reputedly the largest single span ones in the country. Despite the steep hill in between, the village was always loyal to its well-used station. c.1913 The Dartmoor Trust Archive.

An updated view of Old Station Road shows no trace of the railway. A cattle grid marks the site of the level crossing, closed in 1952 when the road was diverted around the hair pin bend to join the A386 about 200 yards further east in 1952, a wicket gate surviving for pedestrian use until closure of the line. 26 April 2017.

A Plymouth-bound train pulling away from Horrabridge up the 1 in 60 grade towards Yelverton. In the foreground, the road is the Tavistock Turnpike which would become the A386 when it was laid out in its present form in 1922. To the top right is the Manor Hotel, today this stands by the 30mph speed restriction board for Horrabridge on the A386 road now amid much development. The date of 1912 supplied for the picture would fit as the train is hauled by one of the early 45XX tanks with the enlarged bunker and its number plate placed centrally on the tank. The stock is a remarkably uniform set from the mid 1880s apart from the odd Dean 3 arc-roof one, which would be about a decade younger. The Dartmoor Trust Archive.

The topography of the land has altered the present day view taken about ten yards or so to the right of the original and probably higher by a few feet The hedge and wall to the left of the two houses in the foreground mark the A386, almost completely lost in the growth to the top right the former Manor hotel still exists, there is no evidence of the railway making its way up the hill. 25 March 2018.

1408 running in to Yelverton with the 1040 Plymouth-Tavistock South, the stock an auto trailer "dia L 70" from 1908, probably series 53-70. At this time the vehicle still retained its top lights (many were sheeted over latterly), it would still have been gas lit and is in BR maroon livery. This is the summit of the line between Plymouth and Tavistock at 500 feet above sea level, the village a further 100 feet above. The line through here had opened in 1859; it passed under the hamlet of Elfordtown in a tunnel ignoring the small population. Save for a goods siding here, Horrabridge was deemed sufficient to serve the local area. The opening of the Princetown branch at first did not aid the cause for a station but eventually one was provided, opening 1 May 1885. The hierarchy of the GWR disliked the name Elfordtown and chose to call their siding, signal box (interior shown right c.1930) and station, Yelverton. The village grew apace with the frequent train service provided; indeed Yelverton was as much a railway creation as Crewe or Swindon. The station site has

The Dartmoor Trust Archive

grown over and public access is not possible or encouraged. So arrival at Yelverton introduces two further notable railways of Dartmoor, their stories partly entwined. 5 July 1955, the late R.C. Riley, The Transport Treasury

The Plymouth & Dartmoor Railway

The Plymouth & Dartmoor was the brainchild of Sir Thomas Tyrwhitt, a notable politician who spent most of his later life and much of his money trying to cultivate and populate Dartmoor, a mission that was not entirely successful as the introduction of agriculture to the High Moor failed. He was main shareholder of the P&D which opened on 26 September 1823 from King Tor to Sutton Pool, the distance between the two by the line 23 miles, as the crow flies 13, the railway following the contours. Built to the gauge of 4'6" which became known as the Dartmoor gauge the route had only one major engineering feature, the 620 yard Leigham Tunnel. The line was said to have cost £66 000 – a considerable sum at the time – but the projected levels of traffic failed to materialise and financial trouble started at once. The company did not have the necessary funds to complete the line to Princetown; this was achieved by John and William Johnson, who were working the quarries in the King Tor/Swell Tor areas and saw the railway as the means of transporting their granite down to Plymouth. The Johnson Bros acquired a mortgage on the P&D, the latter unable to pay interest so the granite travelled toll free. Other traffic was scarce, the P&D not becoming its own master again until June 1865 when an agreement was reached with William Johnson (his brother had since died). Soon it was using the revenue from the granite traffic to relay the line and the upper section beyond Yelverton was sold in 1878 for £22 000 to the Princetown Company, more of which anon, after which the lower section from Yelverton saw occasional traffic until c.1900. To cut a very long story very short, in 1875 the P&D Company became involved with the LSWR in the Plymouth area acting as its agent, firstly obtaining powers for short branch lines in the Cattewater area, and in August 1883 for the Turnchapel Branch which was built under its auspices. These were taken over by the LSWR. The rails from Yelverton to where the Lee Moor Tramway at the Rising Sun (now buried beneath the present day Marsh Mills roundabout and interchange) joined the route were lifted in 1916, the metals going to aid the war effort. The P&D Company managed to exist as a separate identity until the Grouping of 1923 when it was absorbed by the Southern Railway. Subsidiary lines from the P&D will be discussed when we reach the Lee Moor Tramway.

The Princetown Branch

Possibly the most dramatic, scenic and much lamented of all former GWR lines, the standard gauge Yelverton–Princetown Branch opened on 11 August 1883, the service running to and from Horrabridge as there was not a station at the physical junction at Yelverton until the latter station opened 1 May 1885. The route covered much of the upper section of the Plymouth & Dartmoor Railway with some deviations, particularly in the Burrator and Swell Tor areas. The distance from Yelverton to Princetown by road is 6 miles; by train it was 10½ miles, the railway following the contours to gain height, with a spectacular loop to round King Tor. Walking over the moor from the line at the start of the loop by the surviving masonry overbridge, it is a half mile easy climb to reach the track bed at King Tor, yet the train would have to follow a 2½ mile detour climbing 200 feet in the process. On a fine day the view from the train must have been just breathtaking.

Traffic levels were always sparse; prisoners for HMP Dartmoor came by road from the LSWR at Tavistock from 1930, in summer walkers and hikers made good use of the line, but not enough to stave off closure. The branch was extremely susceptible to road competition and was closed completely as from 5 March 1956, being dismantled over the following autumn and winter. The route from Burrator to Princetown is now a foot and cycle path.

Seen from a Tavistock bound train, the snow appears to be crisp and even but not deep in this Edwardian view of a train from Princetown having arrived at Yelverton. The view is looking in the Plymouth direction in March 1914. The 44XX tank has a single Dean Clerestory coach, indicating even then traffic levels were not high. The Dartmoor Trust Archive.

Opposite: Taken looking back from a train heading for Princetown as it is about to traverse the level crossing over Meavy road, here's a view of Dousland station in its final weeks of operation. Upon the opening of the line in 1883, Dousland was the only intermediate station. It was always a block post, in simple layman's terms breaking the line into two single-line token sections, but very rarely was there ever more than one train on the branch at a time. Its 14-lever frame and cramped signal box of 1915 – it was only 10 feet high inside – can be seen on the platform. The points lead to a small goods yard which could be accessed from either end, in effect creating a loop but this was never used to pass trains. The station lay beside the B3212 road and is the only one of the branch which still survives, now in use a private residence. February 1956.

54 chains from Dousland, at Prowse's Crossing the line crossed Iron Mine Lane where the latter met the Meavy road, just by the former Pigeon Post Tea Rooms. The crossing keeper was under the control of Dousland signal box and opposite his hut was a three lever ground frame; two for the distant signals each way and one for locking the crossing. c.1952, Dartmoor Trust Archive.

Iron Mine Lane is a reminder of former industrial activity in the area, and it still plays a part in serving one of the pockets of industry exploiting the mineral resources of Dartmoor as it leads to Yennadon Quarry. There is little evidence of the former level crossing, a residence now occupies the site of the crossing keeper's hut, and the Pigeon Post Tea Rooms are a memory. 5 April 2018.

Named after Albert Prowse at nearby Yennadon House, this early view of Prowse's Crossing shows the signals in place and a signboard advertising 'Teas, Hot Water and Mineral Water' for sale. After the railway's closure the crossing keeper's cottage became Dousland Post Office and Stores for many years.

Burrator and Sheepstor Halt from the goods brake van at the rear of the 1208 Tuesdays, Thursdays and Saturdays only mixed (i.e. passengers and freight) Princetown–Yelverton. Between 1893 and 1898 Burrator and Sheepstor Dams were built to form a reservoir to supply Plymouth, the workmen making their own way from Dousland. In 1923 the dams were extended to increase capacity. Of timber construction supported on trestle legs with cross members and a little waiting shelter, it opened as an unadvertised station for the workmen 4 February 1924 and due to popular demand to the public from 18 May 1925. The view from the carriage window was here was one of the finest in the country; the reservoir is to the right, towering over it is Leather Tor, to the left the Sharpitor mast can be seen on the skyline. Other than the kissing gate at the top of the path from the station, nothing remains of the railway here today, the route here built on a major deviation from that of the P&D. 5 July 1955, the late R.C. Riley, The Transport Treasury.

On the last day of service, two engines and six coaches were needed from the afternoon onwards to accommodate those taking a last sentimental journey. Taken from the carriage window as the train rounds the curve at Routrundle on the climb to Ingra Tor, 4568+4583 double head the six-coach 1451 Yelverton-Princetown, the train running about 35 minutes late due to the complex shunting operations at Yelverton of adding 4583 and three coaches, which had worked up from Plymouth as part of the 1410 to Tavistock South, to 4568 and its three coaches which had worked earlier services that day. 3 March 1956, Ian H. Lane.

Through wide open spaces, the curve at Routrundle seen from above looking from Peak Hill, 4568+4583 and their train would have been on the section where the line takes the left hand turn before making the sharp turn to the right to disappear behind the rocks and make the stop at Ingra Tor Halt. I have included this picture just to illustrate how spectacular was the scenery to be seen from the train to Princetown. Dartmoor at its very best. 27 September 2018.

The cows graze on and take little notice as 4410 pulls away from Ingra Tor Halt with the 1119 Yelverton-Princetown. Had one come from Plymouth to connect with this train, one would have ridden behind 1408 in that ancient auto coach we saw arriving at Yelverton. Ingra Tor Halt, remote with no road access was a good half mile walk over the Moor from the B3212, and was the last station on the branch to open on 2 March 1936. This station was aimed at walkers and hikers; it was useful for the residents of Routrundle Farm. It was also unique in having a notice warning people to keep their dogs on a lead due to the presence of adders in the area. Known as the Ingra Tor snake notice, it is preserved by the PRC in their Lee Moor Tramway Museum at Buckfastleigh. This is just about as wild and remote as the Dartmoor Railway scene would ever get. 5 July 1955, the late R.C. Riley, The Transport Treasury.

The Princetown train, climbing the incline at Kings Tor with Ingra Tor in the background. c.1920. The Dartmoor Trust Archive.

The line passing Swell Quarry, c.1951. The Dartmoor Trust Archive.

A lonely station not too sure of its correct identity; the name board stated this was King Tor Platform, the time table claimed it was King Tor Halt. Both were wrong as the actual nearby hill is known as King's Tor. This remote stopping place opened 2 April 1928 serving a group of quarrymen's cottages and little else, although it was popular with hikers. The view is looking towards Yelverton. Construction was of earthworks topped with gravel and a timber platform lining. This could be a bleak place. Those in the know took advantage of the permanently open door of the nearby permanent way hut. c.1951, The Dartmoor Trust Archive.

The Princetown fixed distant signal with the tower of St Michael and All Angels church in the the far distance herald the end of the journey from Yelverton, c.1951. The Dartmoor Trust Archive.

Final chapter. Dismantling the Princetown railway at milepost 2¾ just to the west of Burrator Platform, 5569 has charge of the track lifting train 20 February 1957. The Dartmoor Trust Archive.

A Chapman's postcard view of the terminus at Princetown: behind the sturdy goods shed, on the platform we get a good view of the main station building, its canopy with large wooden screens at each end to protect the staff and the passengers from the worst of the weather. The houses to the left were built in 1910 and look quite new, and with the publishers early code helps to date this c.1911. Dartmoor Trust Archive.

Behind the trees the tower of St Michael and All Angels still keeps watch. At 1373 feet above sea level, Princetown was the highest station in England and demolished in 1960. The view has two notable additions: to the left North Hessary Tor mast, brought in to use around the time of the closure of the railway, to the right the Dartmoor Brewery, the highest in England built in 2005. 11 April 2018.

Princetown had a third railway, but to be able to visit its southern terminus one needs to be detained at Her Majesty's Pleasure. Not many railways emanated from within a prison making the Omen Beam tramway unique. It was conceived to transport peat from the open Moor for producing naphtha. Two Plymouth businessmen Jacob Hall-Drew and Peter Adams rented Tyrwhitt's Mill at Bachelors Hall to the east of Princetown, moving in 1846 to the then out of use Dartmoor Prison. From here they built a tramway, under the auspices of the British Patent Naphtha Company, in a northerly direction to Yearlick Ball, with a branch to Omen Beam near Fice's Well. The total length was 2¼ miles; the gauge thought to be 4'½" and was horse worked. Its closure date is uncertain; it certainly was in use in the early years of the prison becoming a penal institution in 1850, the rails were lifted during the First War. The route is easily accessed from the B3357 Two Bridges Road east of Rundlestone Corner Grid Ref SX 578750 where the tramway on its clearly defined embankment curves away from the Prison South Gate, this section is out of bounds to the general public. 27 September 2018.

HM Prison Dartmoor. This photograph from 1913 shows some of the many buildings that surrounded the prison's core, within a high stone wall just glimpsed between the buildings in the foreground. In the mid 1840s the British Patent Naptha Company leased part of the prison for the distillation of peat into naptha on a commercial scale. Candles and gas for lighting their premises were among the by-products of this enterprise which lasted only for a few years. The gas holders in the picture reveal that gas was still used for lighting and heating in 1913. The Dartmoor Trust Archive.

Heading north from the Two Bridges Road, the tramway is easily followed. A few yards beyond the third gate from the B3357 the line bends on a very discernable curve, at the start of which one can see the remains of a gas works to the right. Beyond this the signpost marks the path down to the left to Fice's Well, and the eye can follow the tramway back to the road and in the distance see where it began as the Prison acts as an obvious landmark. 27 September 2018.

The line heading towards Black Dunghill, taking a left-hand turn at the end of the shallow cutting. About ½ miles beyond, the track bed peters out in the open moor by Mistor Marsh; the route to the very end is for the more ardent walkers. 27 September 2018.

A return to Yelverton to resume our journey south, initially following the P&D looking along Yelverton Common towards Plymouth; visible in the foreground are the granite sleepers of the P&D. On the A386 the 83 bus makes its way to Tavistock. March 1961, Dartmoor Trust Archive.

Where the line crosses the minor road from the A386 very close to Yelverton Rock, the granite sets are prominent, look very carefully in the left foreground and clearly visible is the only remaining piece of rail. 22 September 2014.

Tyrwhitt's Wharf c.1940.
The Dartmoor Trust Archive

Other than where the track bed is still visible, surviving infrastructure of the Plymouth & Dartmoor is hard to find. On the moor the jewel in the crown can be found on the hill above Clearbrook, where the line curves to cross the road from the A386. Built at almost the mid point of the P&D between the 11 and 12 mileposts, the sturdy stone building was a depot known as Tyrwhitt's Wharf and also served as stables. Here horses were changed, fed and rested. Today it serves as a store for Yelverton Golf Club, saved from impending dereliction as the earlier photograph shows. Further on towards Roborough, the line can be easily followed often with granite sleepers still in place. As one enters Plymouth, this task is not so easy. 22 September 2014.

From Clearbrook we leave the P&D to descend in to the Meavy Valley, but not at this stage to join the Tavistock Branch. We are at Goodameavy – welcome to the railway that never was. Nearby stands the 745 feet Dewerstone: a place of myth and legend, today popular with walkers and rock climbers but which was formerly quarried for its granite. The Johnson brothers, whom we encountered earlier when writing about the P&D, in 1857 cast their eyes on working granite from the Dewerstone, quarrying starting the following year. It was planned to build a siding to link a tram road with the SDR Tavistock Branch on the other side of the river. A cutting was made through solid rock leading to a 200 yard embankment which included a stone bridge to accommodate a riverside track, still visible today as shown in this photograph. On the other side of the river an area of flat ground was created to allow for the proposed interchange siding, with a stone support for the proposed bridge. After all this work had been done, for some inexplicable reason the bridge over the river was never built, one suspects the Johnson brothers may have preferred to lug their granite the mile up hill along the lane to Clearbrook and the P&D, where their stone would travel toll free as opposed to paying the South Devon & Tavistock for the privilege. Parts of the embankment were removed in 1952–54, the spoil being used in the construction of Lopwell Dam. The embankment is fenced off and never saw a train.

The cutting made to link the never completed spur to the SDR to the end of the Tramway, despite its railway like appearance this also never saw a train and remains in use as a footpath. 11 April 2018.

At the end of the cutting is Dewerstone House, the former counting house, smithy and stable, the likely point where steam would have taken over for the onward trip to the Tavistock Branch had the railway that never was been completed, and the start of the tramway which continued up the hill to the right. 11 April 2018.

About ½ mile beyond Dewerstone House, the lower tramway to the left continued to a small former quarry in Dewerstone Wood, met on the right the counter balanced worked incline 400 feet in length with a 1 in 6 gradient that linked to the two quarries on the upper level. Granite sets used instead of sleepers can be seen in a number of places, and are prominent in the foreground here. There are scant remains of the underground drum house at the summit, where the short upper tramway that led to the quarries commenced. Here the plentiful evidence of the two quarries amongst the growth and wilderness are a grim reminder of the industrial past, but the climb is well worth it for the superb views that can still be enjoyed from this vantage point. The quarries ceased working as far as I know in 1878; it is unknown when the track was removed, and there are no known photographs of the quarries or tramway when in use. 11 April 2018.

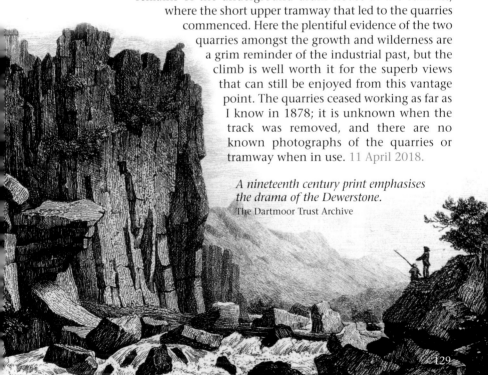

A nineteenth century print emphasises the drama of the Dewerstone.
The Dartmoor Trust Archive

4555 disturbs the peace at Shaugh Bridge Platform with the 1015 from Launceston; the station built on the site of Shaugh Siding which existed from the early 1870's to take iron ore from a nearby mine. 29 September 1962, the late R.C. Riley, The Transport Treasury.

Bickleigh, the epitome of the GWR country station; its setting was superb where Bickleigh Vale and the southern slopes of the Moor meet in the shadow of Bickleigh Down. Here existed a glorious view looking east towards Shaugh Prior and the Dewerstone. A Plymouth-Tavistock South auto train departs. 15 July 1961, the late R.C. Riley, The Transport Treasury.

The Tavistock branch leaves Dartmoor as it drops down through the Plym Valley, where this opens out lay Plym Bridge Platform. This is the third station to have been constructed here, 705 waiting with the 1430 to Marsh Mills. 27 May 2018.

705 shortly after leaving Plym Bridge, passing works for the new Canada Siding, the original a few yards south on the opposite side of the line was installed by the Canadian Forestry Commission for the loading of timber opening 15 February 1918, lasting about 4 years. High above out of sight on the hill to the left ran the Plymouth & Dartmoor; we take a deviation to have a look. 27 May 2018.

Coming from Plym Bridge on Plym Bridge Road is the northern portal of Leigham Tunnel, the most tangible reminder of the P&D. It is 620 yards in length, 9½ feet high and 109 feet beneath the surface at its greatest depth. Disused from 1900 and track removed in the First War, the Second War would grant it a short lease of new life. It was acquired by Plymouth Corporation for use as an air raid shelter in 1941 being fitted as such in early 1943, By November 1944 the threat had passed and it was transferred to the Admiralty to store munitions, this commencing in October 1945. Bringing rails back to the structure, a short thought to be 2 foot gauge tramway was built to just inside the southern portal from a lane off Plym Bridge Lane; its life span unknown but under a decade. The tunnel is now owned (and neglected) by the city of Plymouth, who does not seem to realise what a precious relic they have. It is not possible to walk through it. Pictured here is the southern granite portal, the spoil above the works for the new road system being built for the emerging Leigham housing estate. April 1968.

The Lee Moor Tramway

Geology gave the northern moor hard stone around Meldon; it gave the southern moor china clay. The P&D was unable to finance any of the three branch lines it spurned. The history of these lines is complex, a brief summary: the Cann Quarry branch was, after a legal dispute, built from a junction with the P&D at the Rising Sun Inn opening 20 November 1829 to meet the canal leading from Cann Quarry at Coypool.

This was extended along the towpath in 1834, and lasted until 1900. Transport of china clay to Plymouth by horse and cart on uneven roads was difficult, partly eased when a branch from Marsh Mills was built in 1834 to Plympton, the latter closed when taken over by the South Devon Railway in 1847. The third route again came off the Cann Quarry Branch at a point near to Plym Bridge, this being the Lee Moor Tramway.

It first opened in September 1854 but was built on the cheap by the South Devon & Tavistock as the price for Lord Morley's support. It was closed the following month due to an accident on the Torycombe incline. The rebuilt line reopened 24 September 1858 being becoming the property of William Phillips, the lessee of the Earl of Morley, sold to a Mrs R Martin and to English China Clays in 1919. It rose from the Plym Valley up Cann Wood Incline, thence to Torycombe where a further cable operated incline took the tramway up to Lee Moor. It would appear the extension to Cholwich Town opened at the same time. The latter was closed in 1910.

After 1916 the tramway, together with the remaining parts of the two other lines, were incorporated in to one to allow traffic still to reach the Cattewater, thus becoming the only survivor of the 4'6" Dartmoor gauge. It crossed the GWR on the level in three places, the Tavistock Branch at Lee Moor Crossing, the Coypool Branch now lost under the PVR Marsh Mills site and the main line at Laira

On the Dartmoor gauge line, horse-drawn wagons bound for Lee Moor are hauled past the former GWR Laira Goods Yard c.1945, the site now incorporated into the Laira Diesel Depot. The Dartmoor Trust Archive.

Junction. It was closed in 1939, reopening after the Second War in 1945 principally to return items to Plymouth taken out for storage for the duration of the War. The section above Plym Bridge was closed in 1947 when a pipe line was commissioned to take the clay down to the Marsh Mills. Horse drawn trains used the right of way over Lee Moor Crossing until the Clay Company gave up this section in 1955, continuing from Coypool into Plymouth on a handful of days each year to maintain the right of way until the last ran 26 August 1960. All the Dartmoor gauge lines were horse-worked except for the Lee Moor Tramway where steam locomotives were used between the head of the Cann Wood Incline and Torycombe.

Lee Moor Crossing looking towards Bickleigh; the Tramway route can be picked out diagonally passing over the branch formation from the clutter on the left to the surviving gate post on the right. 10 June 1983.

Remarkably this is the same place 35 years later after restoration by the PVR, incorporating a new level crossing built at a straight rather than diagonal angle to take the cycle path which utilises the former Lee Moor Tramway from Coypool to Plym Bridge, over the rebuilt railway line. 25 March 2018.

About half a mile beyond Cann Wood, the Tramway crossed the Plympton to Shaugh Prior road by a level crossing with traditional gates. This is Whitegates Crossing, the line beyond leading to Truelove Bridge with Lee Moor in the distance, and a reminder of the in hospitality of a Dartmoor winter. The gates have since been removed and only the metal poles survive as a reminder of their former presence. February 1982.

The section from Cann Wood to Torycombe was locomotive worked. Two identical 0-4-0 saddle tanks were built by Peckett of Bristol, Lee Moor No 1 arriving in March 1899 and Lee Moor No 2 in September 1899. Both faced Cann Wood and had their own shed at Torycombe. They last worked in 1947.

Fortunately the clay company declined the overtures of the scrap merchants, and responded favourably to an approach from the PRC regarding their preservation. In 1968 the Lee Moor Tramway Preservation Society commenced a cosmetic restoration of No 2. This was completed and the engine left Torycombe on 17 June 1970. We see the locomotive outside its shed in an industrial setting – by way of being an exhibit at the Mayflower Traction Engine Rally at Chelston Meadow – before finding a new home in a stable at Saltram House. The engine moved again to a separate PRC Museum within the SDR complex at Buckfastleigh arriving 2 November 2001.

Restoration of No 1 then began, with the engine moving to Wheal Martyn China Clay Museum near St Austell on 17 March 1975 where it remains to this day. Thereafter the clay company gifted Lee Moor No 2 to the PRC which had amalgamated with the LMTPS in April 1974. 17 June 1970.

A bonus not envisaged when preservation work commenced was the addition of a tramway wagon. One had been discovered in thick growth beside Cann Wood incline; it had derailed and been wrecked at an unknown date in the 1930s. Its remains were recovered and transported gratis to Torycombe by the clay company, and due much to the hard work undertaken by the late Roy Taylor, the wagon was restored and is the only one to survive. Coupled to No 2, the pair stands outside the back of Torycombe Shed. The wagon accompanied No 2 to both Saltram and Buckfastleigh. 17 June 1970.

This photograph c.1920 of the Lee Moor Torycombe brickworks illustrates the former extent of industrial activity in the area. The Dartmoor Trust Archive.

The Lee Moor Tramway itself spawned a little-known branch, namely the short Wotter Tramway. This ran from a junction at the top of the second Torycombe incline to Wotter clay works, and it is thought to have opened with the rest of the rebuilt tramway on 24 September 1858. A view taken at the summit of the incline which is to the left, note how the gradient drops sharply away, curving away to the right is the embankment of the Wotter Tramway. When the Wotter works changed hands, the tramway ceased to serve it from 1900, the first 150 yards were retained for the dual purposes of serving the quarry at Blackalder Tor and storage for the water tank wagons for the incline. This view is now engulfed by growth. April 1968.

The rails laid in the Shaugh Prior to Cornwood road lead the eye to the track bed curving towards the Cholwich Town terminus marked by the chimney of Cholwich Town kiln. Behind are Shell Top and Penn Beacon. April 1968.

Today shows a much changed scene, the rails in the road gone, Cholwich Town flattened, the spoil heaps removed the area now a gateway for the Lorries that serve the clay works. Only the background hill provides any link between the two images. 2 September 2013.

From Cholwich Town it is 3 miles by road through Cornwood to rejoin the GWR main line at the 309 yard Blachford Viaduct where east-bound trains will now pass along the southern boundary of the National Park. 47 824 *Glorious Devon* has charge of the 0725 Plymouth-Glasgow Central/Aberdeen. 15 June 1989.

Moving to the south side of the viaduct, having just passed through the former Cornwood Station, which was not in the National Park unlike the village it served ½ mile away, the powerful pairing of 60163 *Tornado*+6024 *King Edward I* head 1Z65 1702 Plymouth-Eastleigh rail tour. 25 September 2010.

The main line hugs the edge of the Moor as it passes under the southern Tors. Passing Langham is Class 52 D1029 *Western Legionnaire* with the 12 coach Sunday 1A75 1620 Plymouth-Paddington, the clay tips of Lee Moor form a distant back drop. 3 March 1974.

Ivybridge Signal Box stood on the down side of the line at the Plymouth end of the station. It was opened in 1895 with track improvements in the area, a splendid example of typical GWR architectural practice. 15 December 1973.

We can take an evocative look inside the signal box two days before it closed to allow the Plymouth Panel to take control of the line to the outskirts of Totnes. The 30-lever frame shows up well. A brief layman's guide to the levers: the yellow one nearest the camera the down distant, the one at the far end of the frame the up distant. White indicates spare levers, chevrons for laying detonators, red are for signals, black for points and blue for facing point locks. Above is the block shelf with the block bells and instruments, the plungers are an electrical release for certain levers, the round boxes indicating a signal arm or point position. Outside we see my little 100E Ford Car in front of the substantial goods shed. This opened with the goods yard 1 October 1911 to replace the cramped one to the east of Stowford Bridge. This remained open until November 1965 with a railway cartage delivery van and driver based there from the Parcels Depot at Plymouth, and despite no trains stopping at Ivybridge since 1959, the staff held a stock of paper tickets and were able to issue tickets to travel from other stations. The signal box was demolished soon after closure, the goods shed survives in industrial use. 15 December 1973.

A train arrives from Plymouth at the first Ivybridge Station. Opened 15 June 1848, the curved platform extended to the west end of the timber viaduct. The line through the station was doubled in June 1893 when the down platform was constructed. c.1908, The Dartmoor Trust Archive.

Classic SDR architecture, the original Brunel chalet style building of 1848 at the eastern end of the up platform, this became redundant when the station closed to passengers 2 March 1959. No effort was made to preserve this gem and it was demolished with the station in the early 1960s. 1959, The Dartmoor Trust Archive.

143

To the east of the original station, trains cross the River Erme on the 229 yard nine arch built of rock faced granite with blue engineering bricks Ivybridge viaduct, maximum height 104 feet. The white notice in the field is a clue to why this angle is now impossible, the first sign of the housing developers. March 1982.

The rear of the train is just coming off Ivybridge Viaduct, which brings us back to Stowford Bridge to complete the circular tour of Dartmoor by train. 43163 leading and 43145 on the rear provide the power for 1A83 0954 Penzance-Paddington. Hope you have enjoyed the trip! 26 July 2014.